Wedding Chic

THE SAVVY BRIDE'S GUIDE
TO GETTING MORE
WHILE SPENDING LESS

Nina Willdorf

author of
City Chic: An Urban Girl's Guide to Livin' Large on Less

A • PERIGEE • BOOK

A PERIGEE BOOK
Published by the Penguin Group
Penguin Group (USA) Inc.
375 Hudson Street, New York, New York 10014, USA
Penguin Group (Canada), 10 Alcorn Avenue, Toronto, Ontario M4V 3B2, Canada
(a division of Pearson Penguin Canada Inc.)
Penguin Books Ltd., 80 Strand, London WC2R 0RL, England
Penguin Group Ireland, 25 St. Stephen's Green, Dublin 2, Ireland (a division of Penguin Books Ltd.)
Penguin Group (Australia), 250 Camberwell Road, Camberwell, Victoria 3124, Australia
(a division of Pearson Australia Group Pty. Ltd.)
Penguin Books India Pvt. Ltd., 11 Community Centre, Panchsheel Park, New Delhi—110 017, India
Penguin Group (NZ), Cnr. Airborne and Rosedale Roads, Albany, Auckland 1310, New Zealand
(a division of Pearson New Zealand Ltd.)
Penguin Books (South Africa) (Pty.) Ltd., 24 Sturdee Avenue, Rosebank, Johannesburg 2196,
South Africa

Penguin Books Ltd., Registered Offices: 80 Strand, London WC2R 0RL, England

Excerpt from *Buff Brides* by Sue Fleming, copyright © 2001 by Sue Fleming, used by permission of
Villard Books, a division of Random House, Inc.

"Brides One Week Countdown" from *The Nearly Wed Handbook* by Dan Zevin, copyright © 1999, has
been reprinted by permission of HarperCollins Publishers, Inc.

PRINTING HISTORY
Perigee trade paperback edition / January 2005

PERIGEE is a registered trademark of Penguin Group (USA) Inc.
The "P" design is a trademark belonging to Penguin Group (USA) Inc.

Library of Congress Cataloging-in-Publication Information

Willdorf, Nina.
    Wedding chic : the savvy bride's guide to getting more while spending less / Nina Willdorf.—
Perigee trade pbk. ed.
        p. cm.
    ISBN: 0-399-53064-9
    1. Weddings—Planning. 2. Budgets, Personal. I. Title.

HQ745.W54 2005
395.2'2—dc22

                                                                                    2004057681

PRINTED IN THE UNITED STATES OF AMERICA

1   2   3   4   5   6   7   8   9   10

Most Perigee Books are available at special quantity discounts for bulk purchases for sales promotions,
premiums, fund-raising or educational use. Special books, or book excerpts, can also be created to fit
specific needs.

For details, write: Special Markets, The Berkley Publishing Group, 375 Hudson Street, New York, New
York 10014.

FOR MICHAEL

THE THANKS . . .

This book really feels like a team effort. From inception to completion, it would have been virtually impossible without the following people, for whom I feel so thankful to have had the honor to work with.

My researcher, Marisa Milanese, whose intrepid research skills and enthusiasm for the cause reached such heights that she proposed to a lucky man named Mo while interviewing beauty pros about hair and makeup. This book is undeniably better because of you. Ted Moncreiff, for pointing me to Marisa—and for sharing your always-thoughtful advice. My talented illustrator Bonnie Dain, for managing to perfectly translate my voice into drawings. And for enduring round after round of revisions with true patience.

My agent Andrew Stuart, for never failing to pump me up when I start to deflate, and for sifting through my most embarrassing drafts with an emotionally generous red pen. Sheila Curry Oakes, Michelle Howry, and the folks at Perigee books, for taking me on and truly showing me love. Sarah Palmer, for being the most talented shutterbug (among many other things) I know.

Sari Globerman, for being my best reader, devoted friend, and always reliable conscience. You kept me sane during my wedding planning (a virtually impossible feat) and during book writing (another virtually impossible feat). I am truly lucky to have you in my life.

My parents, Lilian Offner and Todd and Judy Endelman, for joining forces to throw one truly chic affair.

Mindy Berry and Iris Sutcliffe, for always being game to read pages and help me choose illustrations and brainstorm titles. You foster my creativity . . .

And to the wonderful team who generously shared their experiences and expertise: Karmen Butterer, Jean Chatzky, Colin Cowie, Yolanda Crous, Dana Dickey, Tara Duggan, Bill Epstein of Nurseryman's Exchange, Frédéric Fékkai, Lynn Harris, Donna Heiderstadt, Amanda Hesser, Sheryl Julian, Carolyn Jung, Megan Kaplan, Kara Corridan, Jane Ko, Nathan Lump, Wendy Perrin, Ilene Rosenzweig, Clea Simon, Amy Sohn, Joel Stein, Paula Szuchman, David Tutera, Sylvia Weinstock, the girls on the board at WeddingChannel.com, and countless others. I—and brides-to-be—will always owe you a debt of gratitude for your honest stories, crisp opinions, and wealth of information.

CONTENTS

PART III

The Post-Wedding Bliss

Wedding Chic

INTRODUCTION

Welcome to the Most Beautiful Day of Your Life!
That'll be $22,000, please.

Congratulations! He popped the question. And after approximately five minutes of elation, certain other questions started to pop: When? Where? And, most important, *Who is going to pay for all of this?!*

Sure, for the most momentous occasion in your life so far, focusing on the practical matter of dollars and cents seems a little petty. That is, until you start discovering just what things cost. Even the simplest wedding can come with a table rental fee of a few thousand dollars. You want a beauty pro to work her magic on your hair? Try $200 an hour, with a two-hour minimum. You'd like to have your wedding dress professionally dry-cleaned after the event? Better squirrel away as much as $400. Even having that chuppah delivered to the temple could set you back a few hundred bucks. Things are starting to look not so romantic, huh?

Every girl begins the wedding planning process thinking that she wants to keep things simple—low-key. And slowly . . . gradually . . . seeds begin to sprout: The dress grows a train; the friends of friends go from B-List to A-List and your guest count balloons; the flower budget defies pruning; the meal bloats with an extra course.

And the budget that you set—$1,000, $10,000, or $100,000—begins to grow, slowly but surely. Consider your engagement to be a crash course in a new kind of bargain hunting. The learning curve is steep—because you generally have about sixteen months to learn the ins and outs of the wedding industry. Fondant frosting, calla lilies, chignon, A-line, and artistry package are just some of the terms that will be thrown at you in the next few months.

At the same time, the stakes are high; your wedding is far more expensive than any shopping splurge you've ever made. The wedding industry is an enormous affair that thrives on a necessarily captive and green audience. Not many of us go through it more than once, and unless you're a party planner by trade, the nuts and bolts of planning a big bash will be all new to you. But even if your budget is more Bellagio than backyard, every engaged girl's goal is the same: to pull off a beautiful, special, and unique event. You want to squeeze the most chic out of every penny, to negotiate the best contracts, to dig into the heart of the matter and find the pearl in the rough. The truth is, it is possible to have the wedding you want on the budget you have.

I recently emerged from the haze of planning my wedding in the San Francisco Bay Area. At one point I was sifting through quotes from at least six makeup artists who were all in the $200-an-hour range, my venue coordinator insisted that we absolutely *must* go with the tablecloth covered in green leaves for the cake table (*who was running this show?*), my florist conveniently forgot that he had promised to include pedestals for our flowers, and my expenses kept creeping up.

When people inspected my ring, gushing, "Isn't it all so exciting?" I could only nod slowly and wonder if they ever had to negotiate with a printer about prices for ink colors. *Fabulous!* Unfortunately, this is all part of the reality of planning "The Most Beautiful Day of Your Life."

By the Numbers

Before you head out into the Wild World of Wedding Planning with a sparkly new ring on your finger and a sign that says "sappy sucker," it's helpful to know what other girls around the country have paid, on average. That way you can know if you're getting a deal or getting duped. (Note: Prices generally run higher in metropolitan areas.)

Average cost for day of hair/makeup	$357
Average cost of invitations	$381
Average price for a wedding dress	$799
Average cost for a wedding DJ	$400 to $2,000
Average cost of wedding flowers	$967
Average cost for a wedding planner	$1,500 to $6,000
Average cost for wedding photographs	$1,814
Average amount spent on honeymoon	$3,471
Average cost of food, drinks, and venue rental	$7,360
Average cost for wedding band	$1,300 to $10,000

Source: Condé Nast Bridal Infobank, publishers of *Bride's* and *Modern Bride* magazines; Claudia Hanlin, New York Wedding Library; TheKnot.com.

By no means did I have what could be considered a low-budget wedding. Just as I sometimes splurge on shoes or haircuts but scrimp on other areas, I was mindful from the beginning about where I wanted to devote my dollars. And I decided to spend a lot on a few important items: I paid more than $2,000 for a beautiful ivory gown; I spent more than $2,000 on flowers; and I spent about $1,000 on invitations and all the parts of the printing package.

Throughout the process, whether I was splurging or scrimping, I was keen on making sure I was being as budget-savvy as I could be without getting the tulle pulled over my eyes. Whether I was negotiating linen rental costs, searching out the lowest airfare for the honeymoon, or buying my own fabulous wedding-day makeup at a department store, I wanted to be certain that I was getting the best value for my money. The fact is, whatever amount you have to spend on your wedding, you want the money to stretch as far as it can to afford you the best, most stylish, and reliable services.

The whole time I was planning my wedding, I was constantly searching for guidance, for books that would make sense of this new lingo and, more important, give me the straight scoop on how to maximize my dollars. I craved a crash course, some CliffsNotes, secret tips, and short cuts. I wanted someone to let me know that dressmakers often tack on a hefty surcharge for lace dresses; that hydrangeas are in season in the summer on the West Coast, making them a wonderfully affordable option; that I should never—*never*—accept the first price that anyone quotes; that I should ask my photographer early on about buying my negatives; and that serving trout instead of sea bass could save me 50 percent on my catering costs.

There was so much to learn in such a short time, and the only place where I could find the real cost-saving scoop was through recently married friends who were practically bursting with their desire to unload some of the wisdom that they had painstakingly acquired—often at an excessive cost. It was a sisterhood of married women, bubbling over with tips for the newbies. "Someone else should at least profit from my research!" they would say.

That is what I have done with *Wedding Chic.* Through hundreds of interviews with caterers, florists, musicians, bartenders, photographers, venue coordinators, newlyweds, and wedding and event planners, I've assembled the most comprehensive cost-saving guide to squeezing the most style out of any wedding budget. I've written the book that I wish I had when I was planning my own wedding. Whatever your budget may be, you're looking to make it work for you, and this book will help you do just that.

Wedding Chic is your right-hand girlfriend, helping you keep an eye on the bottom line, teaching you how to ask for what you want, steering you toward the best services, and guiding you away from the worst. Throughout the book, you'll find regular features with mini helpful tips ("Who Knew?"), valuable nuggets of advice ("Word to the Wise"), and tip-offs of unnecessary charges ("Hidden Cost"). You'll find seasonal flower guides to help you choose the best-priced blooms for your wedding, the real deal about alteration costs, simple food substitutions to shave your catering costs, and a global guide to finding the best location with both ideal weather and good deals on your honeymoon, among countless other useful features. The book is organized from the beginning of the wedding process (deciding if you need a wedding planner, selecting invitations) to day-of events (choosing flowers, entertainment, and food), to the forever after (planning the honeymoon). You can pick it up at any spot for useful information, or you can use it to guide you through every step of the planning process.

It may not seem so romantic to be thinking constantly about the bottom line. *Isn't a wedding just about love, fun, and fabulousness?* But the surest way to set yourself up for the most unromantic situation is to rack up years' worth of debt in order to pay for a flock of white doves and a horse and carriage. There is no reason that having "the wedding of your dreams" has to cause financial nightmares for years to come.

Remember, this is just one day in your entire life together. It should be meaningful and special, and it will be because of the ceremony you are participating in together. It's important to remember, throughout all the inevitable contract negotiations, family dueling, and tiffs with your fiancé, what this whole affair is about: the union of two people who love each other very much and want to have a ceremony to celebrate their commitment with family and friends in attendance.

There may be countless times throughout the planning process, as you become mired in work, family, and planning this big bash, that you may feel like you're simply going to burst. This is normal. You may scream, cry, or threaten to elope. This is normal, too. Earmark this page, so that when things get hairy you can take a moment, regain your sanity, and refresh your memory about the following key guidelines.

Wedding Chic Maxims

You're running the show. Don't get bullied by anybody else.

Whatever it is, it's not that important.

There will be life after the wedding (and honeymoon).

The wedding is for you and your fiancé—not your guests. Focus on what you want; don't obsess about what everyone attending will want or need.

The customer is always right. Don't let vendors tell you it has to be any other way.

Enjoy yourself.

Part 1

THE PRE-WEDDING PLANNING

"People get very stuck in that wedding formula; it's the same thing—a five-hour party where everything so traditional is incorporated within that celebration. That's what escalates the budget very quickly. You can do something unique and unusual, and it winds up being less expensive."

DAVID TUTERA
EVENT PLANNER • NEW YORK CITY

1 · Do You Need a Wedding Planner?

hile you've always been the resident expert at scoring deals on designer shoes, asking "pretty please" for a discount on furniture delivery, or batting an eyelash for a free cocktail, all of a sudden you find yourself swimming in completely new territory. Weddings! They sound so fabulous. They are an iconic American fantasy. You can close your eyes and see flower petals, cloth-covered chairs, a big white dress, and you and your new husband twirling on a dance floor. But what goes into pulling one off? Unless you're a second-time bride, this is completely new territory. Band vs. DJ? Buffet vs. sit-down? Hotel vs. restaurant? White vs. ecru? The questions can be mind-boggling.

It's difficult to determine what the best choices are. This is bound to be a period when you have to make myriad decisions, and make them fast. Even the most capable multitaskers among us can use a little assistance.

Because I didn't have a background in corporate party planning or public relations, even conceiving of how to start planning my event for 120 people left me flopping on the couch, tossing my hands up in the air. I was absolutely thrilled at the prospect of getting married to my then-fiancé, Michael, but it was hard for me to envision the path from slipping on an engagement ring to walking down the aisle. How would I find the right florist? Where would the wedding be? What kind of food would we serve? How much should we allocate for each service and vendor? How much should my dress cost? I was paralyzed by how little I knew.

While calling all your friends may help, you also might want to consider hiring a pro to come in and play the angel on your shoulder, whispering apropos directions, negotiating with vendors—and your parents—and simply saying "there, there" when emotions inevitably start to run high. Before you commit to getting help, you should know what to expect.

Wedding Consultant vs. Wedding Coordinator

There are two basic kinds of wedding planners: consultants and coordinators. There is a world of difference between the two, both in price and in the level of service they provide.

A consultant: advises you beforehand on particular facets of the process, such as which vendors to use, how to structure the timing of the event, and even how to deal with misbehaving family members.

A coordinator: holds your hand from beginning to teary end, from I Will (Marry You) to I Do (Take You).

Consider a Coordinator or Consultant

While some of us have time to pound the pavement and search for the absolute best cake baker, seamstress, and fabric store, there are moments when a girl just needs to admit that she could use some extra help. Swamped at work, cramming on deadlines, or even planning an event from 3,000 miles away can all make a wedding seem unmanageable. You should seriously consider calling in reserves in the following situations:

1. You live far away from where you plan to have your wedding.

2. You're new to the area and are at a loss for where to start in planning an enormous event.

3. You work in the kind of job where every personal call requires you to take your cell phone into the street.

Wedding Planners: What Can You Do for Me Lately?

*I*t sounds so wonderfully dreamy to delegate all the dirty work to someone else. Can you envision it? A chic lady will arrive on your doorstep, and in one fell swoop, she will find the perfect three-piece fusion jazz/funk/rock/hip-hop band that will both blow away the twentysomethings and appease the sixtysomethings; she will personally hand-address your invites; she will expertly mediate with Mom; she will winningly prod your caterer to make exactly what you want for the same price as the low-budget pasta dish she was trying to pawn off; and then she will discreetly shampoo your carpet in her spare time. OK, it's time to wake up and deal with the reality.

The best wedding planner is one part personal coach, one part contract negotiator, one part Best Friend Forever, one part fashion stylist, one part therapist, and one part researcher. You have to remember that you're not hiring a personal assistant. You need to manage your expectations. What exactly can a wedding consultant or coordinator do for you? Here's a realistic portrait of the tasks you can outsource in the best of all worlds:

• **The detective work.** A good planner will know your local wedding industry like the back of her well-manicured hand. She'll float into the best shops and be greeted with awe, respect, and special deals. A good planner can lead you to places you might not find in the phone book, bridal magazines, or the message boards you've been trolling for tips. She is clued in to the best secret services before you even make her acquaintance. Sure enough, the best of 'em act like a concierge at the Ritz; one fast flip through the old Rolodex reveals the perfect venue for you, and the contact information of the caterer who is listed nowhere.

• **The dirty work.** Some of us couldn't pay a high enough price just to have someone else read through the fine print. With weddings, there is plenty of it—be-cause you will want to have contracts with all of your vendors, from parking valets to the florist for the rehearsal dinner. A planner, however demure he or she may appear, has plenty of stern looks behind that smile. To fight for your best interests and weed out any possible scam, she can go from sweet to scary in a matter of minutes.
Bewildering contracts? *No problem!* Hidden add-on costs? *Unearthed before you put your pen to the paper!* A vendor drops out at the last minute? *Think again, buddy! We read the fine print, and that's not kosher at this wedding.*

• **The director's work.** Coordinating a mass event is no minor feat; it requires someone with the skills of the most polished diplomat, and who can quietly but effectively make things happen while operating behind the scenes. With a wave of the hand, the valets get tipped, the hairdresser is waiting when you arrive at the hotel, the band knows where to be and when, the flowers are arranged just so, and everyone's lapel is perfectly crisp. The director frees you from all concern about even the smallest details, enabling you to focus on your honey's fine face at the altar, rather than the fact that your bridesmaid's dress is utterly wrinkled.

- **The haggler's work.** Although planners cost money, it can be argued that you will ultimately save more money using one than by not doing so. This is because a good planner will use her savvy and experience to negotiate the best deals for you. To start, a planner can help you come up with a bud-

How to Break Down Your Budget

Although a planner may be able to help you assemble a budget, it's helpful for those going solo to know the nuts and bolts of how you should allocate your pennies. The following is an approximate rule of thumb for major expenses.

Beauty costs (hair, makeup)	2 percent
Invitations and stationery	3 percent
Flowers	5 percent
Photographs	8 percent
Attire and accoutrements	10 percent
Music	10 percent
Miscellany (officiant, favors, licenses, tips, etc.)	11 percent
Honeymoon	16 percent
Food and drink	35 percent

get that works for you, and then she can help you get the best prices to meet that budget. One consultant boasts, "I have a couple getting married in October and they are saving four dollars a head on their food costs, ten percent on total rentals, and ten percent on florals." How? A well-connected planner knows instantly just who in the area is looking to promote his or her services or products and therefore may be willing to tack on booking incentives, like free upgrades or discounts. For example, she might be able to negotiate a free engagement photo from your photographer or an extra hour from your musicians.

• **The therapist's work.** A planner's work is never done. When you find yourself meekly asking, "Is this normal?" you will have an ally who can tell you, "Yes, it is. Everyone feels frustrated, alienated, irritated, infuriated, or taken advantage of." Let's face it, you are Bride #4125—so what may feel like a Crazy, Novel, Unique Experience is actually par for the course for this pro. That could be a good thing. Your last-minute zit? "Normal; try toothpaste," she might suggest. Your mom's last-minute freakout? "Normal; take a timeout and have tea to smooth things over," she'll offer. You start to freak yourself out: Is he the one? "Normal; have a romantic evening at home and rediscover why you're doing this in the first place," she'll instruct.

Wedding Planners:
Is the Price Right?

*N*o matter how nice it would be to have someone assume control of the dirty work, narrowing down the choices so that you can roll in to make the final, glorious decisions ("A lighter shade of crème, please! . . . ah-ah, we must have canapés!"), it might not be financially feasible for some of us. Help comes with a price. The question is: How much?

The fee structures for wedding planners fall into three general categories. The prices vary, depending on your location (Peoria's prices aren't the same as, say, Paris). The following are some sample ranges to give you a sense of what things often cost:

- **Flat fees:** From $1,500 to $6,000—and up.

- **Percentage fees:** From 10 to 25 percent of the overall budget.

- **Package fees:** This is like an à la carte menu. You can hire a consultant for a specific task, just a day, or a series of appointments. Here is what you can expect to pay:

Hourly: $50 and up.
Daily: About $600 and up.
Specific Services: From $350 for a two-hour, on-site meeting to generate creative ideas and negotiate with a vendor and create a vendor contact list, a budget summary, and a timeline.

Wedding Chic Word to the Wise: Percentage-Based Fees

*P*ercentage-based fees can raise many an eyebrow. If a coordinator is making money based on your overall budget, wouldn't she be inclined to lead you to the fanciest purchases? Or so goes the cynical thinking. If you find a fantastic person—who knows how firm and unbudgable your budget is—this shouldn't be a concern. If possible, however, try to negotiate for a flat fee or package fee to avoid any problems.

Score! The Best Planner for Your Pennies

*I*f your relationship with your fiancé is number one in the wedding hierarchy, your relationship with your family is number two, and your relationship with your bridal party is number three, your relationship with your coordinator falls somewhere in the midst of your VIPs. She's key.

Why? Everything else in this process has the potential to become complicated. You had your shoes dyed and now

Who Knew?

Even if hiring a pro to walk you through the process is out of the question, you might want to consider à la carte services. Simply getting the names of excellent vendors for a few hundred dollars could make your life that much easier. Be sure to ask the planner if you could meet for a consultation to jump-start your planning and get a list of recommended vendors. The most it should cost you is a couple hundred dollars. The recommendations could save you time—and much money—throughout the process.

they don't fit. There's an airline strike right before your destination wedding in Greece. An unseasonable freeze eliminates the whole crop of artichokes you were planning to use for your first course. The best coordinator sees these as minor obstacles, easily solved. It's worth it to spend a little time at the outset to find someone who can lighten your load rather than piling on more.

To that end, you should be screening a consultant like you do dog walkers, housecleaners, and potential dates. You decide who works for you. Screen potential planners extremely carefully. Find out who you feel comfortable with, who puts you at ease, and who is a good listener. Put serious time into the selection process be-

cause if you end up with a dud, you'll spend money on something (and someone) that could add to your headache.

If you decide to call in a coordinator or consultant as reserves, how do you find your right-hand woman? Two major national professional organizations can help you find a coordinator in your area:

1. The Association for Wedding Professionals International: www.afwpi.com; (800) 242-4461.

2. The Association of Certified Professional Wedding Consultants: www.acpwc.com; (408) 528-9000.

Once you've settled on three or four candidates whom you'd like to interview, you should know what to ask them. First, find out their credentials. If some of your contenders brag about having graduated from the College of All Things Wedding with honors in 1978, find out exactly what that means. Some wedding-credential organizations only require a two- to four-day course, which doesn't really do you much good—especially if it was completed when wedding fashion lived and died by lime-green taffeta gowns. Alternatively, the Association of Certified Professional Wedding Consultants requires applicants to complete hours of coursework and have at least six weddings under their belt before they'll certify them.

Second, ask for references from other couples—and call them! Ask them everything. If you say "chuppah" and they say "huh?" or if you say "unity candle" and they say "umm," it's time to move on. You need someone who speaks the same language, whether or not they've done five Kennedy weddings. Finally, find out exactly how many weddings they're currently planning. If you're paying someone to be your wing woman, you want to feel like priority #1 at all times. Make sure they will be available to you at the drop of a hat—or a tear.

Who Knew?

Newlyweds are often eager to share their well-worn research, so why not put them to use? Hire a recently married acquaintance to be your "day-of coordinator," to make sure the trains run on time at your wedding, to get everyone in the right place at the right time, to manage all of the vendor drop-offs, to pay all the people you've hired, and to do everything you'd rather not do. The cost for this service can range between $50 and $200, depending on how well you know the person. Or instead of paying someone to be your coordinator, swap services with another engaged friend. Dana, a magazine editor in New York City, had two publicist friends volunteer to be her wedding planners. She counted on them for all sorts of things, "from rushing out to buy me a planning book to agreeing to act as the go-to people on the day of that vendors approached as they tried to squeeze more money out of the wedding party." "I'll do yours if you do mine. Deal!"

The Contract Basics

*B*efore signing, make sure the following points are addressed in your contract:

- The date and time of your event (if it is known yet).

- The name and contact info for the planner and yourself.

- The type of service that will be rendered (i.e., package deal or hourly consultancy). Make sure the contract is as specific as possible.

- A specific outline of fees and how the coordinator charges (i.e., as a percentage or flat fee).

- If there is a "price-escalation" clause, which factors in flexibility for additional unforeseen expenses, be sure it is capped no higher than 15 percent.

- The refund policy.

The Bottom Line

- Decide if you need to hire help in your planning.

- Learn the basic difference between wedding consultants and coordinators.

- Figure out the basics of your budget, and what is reasonable to spend on each service or item.

- Become acquainted with everything the coordinator or consultant can and should do for you.

- Decode the wedding planners' fees.

- Find the planner who is the best match for you.

- Consider some creative options.

2 · The Invitations:
Share the Who, What, and Where, for the Right How Much

*A*fter too many nights giving your all to make it past behemoth bouncers guarding "the list" in front of clubs, it's now your turn to play the gatekeeper and assemble your very own VIP list.

While you may have fantasized about a painless process, let's face it, prioritizing friends, parents' friends, and peripheral guests is never easy. Steel yourself now: People will get hurt, people will assume their invitation is "plus one" when it isn't, and someone may just ask if she can request a furlough for her son in juvie to make it to your elegant twenty-one-and-over dinner-and-dancing affair. When in doubt, say no.

As you plan your wedding, it's important to remember that a small guest list will keep your costs down from the beginning to the end. The fact is that one of the easiest ways to control your wedding budget is to limit the guest list. More people = more plates = more tablecloths = more invites = more *everything*. And the prices add up fast! That may seem obvious in the abstract sense, but the costs carry over in unlikely ways. For example, how many gifts will you have to provide for your guests? How many place cards will you need? How many slices of cake? How many chairs, linens, plates, and tablecloths will you need to rent? Adding eight people could require setting up a new table, with an additional set of rentals, another centerpiece, and more chairs. All told, eliminating twenty nonessential people could save you thousands of dollars.

Deciding on your guest list is one of the first—and most important—things you should do. The number of people who will be witness to your nuptials is the single most important factor in your wedding budget. From the start, I fancied a number around 120 (forty for us, forty for my folks, and forty for his folks). Large families and lots of important friends made that fantasy not feasible, and we invited 160, more than the space we'd already rented could comfortably accommodate. Fortunately, we experienced a very common wedding phenomenon: the magic number. More seasoned brides assured me that although we invited 160 people, it was highly unlikely that everyone would say yes. In fact, we could expect to get no's from between 10 and 30 percent of our invitees. Sure enough, by the end of the process, we hit our magic number: 120. The prediction worked, as exactly 25 percent of our invited guests declined.

Whatever your dream number is, and whatever the process of getting there has been (raging fights with your parents, slightly squelched fights with his), you've finally settled on a feasible list. You've accounted for the fact that between 10 and 30 percent of your invitees will politely decline. You've sorted out the A-listers, the B-listers, the no-way-they're-making-it-on-the-listers. You've ranked the camp friends, the "frenemies," the friends of your par-

Word to the Wise
Ranking Your Family and Friends

If you're truly struggling for ways to cut your list, these are some handy guidelines:

1. Only invite couples who live together or who are married. Nix the "plus guest" unless you actually know the name of the guest.

2. Invite people whom you want to be a part of your future together, not necessarily people who were part of your past, which is to say, new friends may have more of a place at your wedding than freshman dorm buddies whom you feel a vague obligation to invite.

ents, your coworkers, his coworkers, your old neighbors, your exes, his exes, your current landlord, your mortgage broker, and your kindergarten teacher (*But she was so special!*). You've swapped your first boyfriend for his former nanny. You've called in agents and lawyers to broker the deals. And now, praise the Lord, you have your list.

The Paper Package

*E*ven without ordering extras such as gold print, embossing, and hand-delivery, your invitation budget can quickly spiral out of control. You might walk into a stationery shop with simple demands, but once you take a look at their sample books of invites (from table cards to thank-you notes), complete with fancy fonts, creative colors, elaborate overlays, and streamlined components, that singular rectangular affair you had in mind may seem a lot less appealing. Invitations aren't one-pagers with envelopes. The whole package is a beguiling affair that will quickly have you rethinking all your preconceived notions about what you thought you wanted. The printed components in a sample wedding package—beyond invitations and envelopes—that could tempt you at the stationery store include:

"Save the date" cards

Place cards

Donation cards

Direction sheets

Hotel information sheets

Menu cards

Ceremony programs

Rehearsal invitations

"In case of rain" cards

Post-wedding brunch invitations

Shower invitations

Social announcements

Thank-you notes

Reading that list may increase your heart rate, similar to the panic induced by thumbing through the latest bridal magazine. *Oh my God, my wedding is going to be a complete disaster if I don't hand-tie gold silk ribbons printed with our names to the bottom of each hand-blown wineglass!* Of course, most of the above paper products are either non-essential or easy to scale down in lower-cost ways than having them all engraved in ecru at Crane's.

Paper Products: Which Should Make the Cut?

*E*ngagement notices: Unless you're a deb, your last name is Rockefeller, or you hail from Savannah, these old-school relics fall into the category of above and beyond. Pick up the phone, and consider that your "engagement notice."

"Save the date" cards: While the older generation might say these are bogus and unnecessary, these cards can be useful if you are inviting folks who will need to travel long distances. A simple, elegant postcard announcing the who, what, and where (just the city will do) will give your friends ample time to request vacation time, make travel arrangements, and forget everything by the time the invitation comes. If you'd like to save more money, enclose all the nitty-gritty logistical information, like which hotels you've blocked, maps, and fun local activities. Though it may require more work earlier in the process, it's cheaper to mail this information along with your "save the date" card than with your invitation, because invitations tend to be heavier and, therefore, postage is pricier.

Keep in mind that "save the date" cards don't have to be elaborate in order to be elegant. Michael and I had fifty postcards printed up at Papyrus, a national paper store chain, to send to our friends. I popped in at the store one day during my lunch hour, quickly flipped through a book, and found the simplest postcard for one of the cheapest prices. A few days later I picked up fifty cards, which we only sent to the young folks. The font was crisp and black, the paper stock was thick, and the fans went wild, raving about our clean, "modern" design. Total cost? $60. Alternatively, a nice note printed at home on thick colored paper can be a wonderfully low-cost way to get the early word out for less than $10.

Invitations: Obviously, there can be no chic wedding if there are no guests. And there will be no guests if people are not invited. Invitations are an unavoidable—and worthwhile—expense. They are also one place that you may choose to splurge, as they begin setting the aesthetic tone for your wedding. Like photographs, they will remain a cherished memento long after the honeymoon is over. (And, no, e-vites are not an option here. Tangible paper has a place in people's hearts.)

RSVP cards: These are an absolutely necessary component for your invitation. If you're completely strapped for cash, you can direct people to e-mail you their RSVP, although then you'll miss out on the warm and witty things people jot down in response to their invitation. Our favorite? My grandmother's response: "If I have to crawl on all fours, I'll be there."

Using a postcard instead of a notecard with an envelope will save you $.17 per RSVP card in postage costs, as well as printing costs for additional envelopes, as all return cards must include a stamp when they are sent out with the invitations. Add it all up, and the simple switch from notecard to postcard could save you at least $17 for 100 invites. It may seem like chump change, but as you embark on the consumer circus act that is the Modern American Wedding, you'll soon realize that every $17 counts. "We had people return the RSVPs on postcards that we'd been saving for years from different trips," notes Joanne Nerenberg, an independent video producer in New York City. "It was fun to choose who got which card. We also printed all our own table seating cards with funny names for tables. Our house became a printing house the week before the wedding. And I spent a lot of time at Kinko's, doing lamination."

Programs: Sure, having your wedding programs printed in letterpress might be stunning, but can't you think of other places you'd rather devote those dollars? Designer Reni Schriek, who runs a design company called TruSo, based in Southern California, says she rarely prints programs anymore. A seven-page program, she notes, can cost just as much as an invitation. Her advice? Create a program that multitasks in an innovative way. For example, for an outdoor wedding, she printed programs on paper fans. Another interesting idea would be to print one large program at the entrance to the ceremony hall. Everyone will see it as they walk in.

If you're wedded to the idea of individual programs, try doing them yourself. Michael's mom made up our wedding programs using Microsoft Word on her home computer and taking a document to Kinko's. A simple program is a task that any craft-impaired person can handle easily. An expensive card stock at Kinko's (ivory executive) will set you back $.27 a sheet. So if you copy 100 programs you've designed yourself on the computer, your entire budget will be a slim $36. Copy, fold, distribute, and collect compliments.

Reception card: Forget it. Just print a one-liner at the bottom of the invitation.

Rehearsal invitations: Bride, meet the phone. Phone, meet bride.

Menus: One expense you need not swallow. People won't even notice the absence.

Maps and hotel and travel information: If you choose not to enclose them with a "save the date," simply print up one info sheet on vellum (so light!) with all relevant information. Or have a wedding website created for you and direct guests there on the bottom of your invitation. As long as the website costs less than printing and postage costs for additional sheets, it can be worth it. (You can get a free website through TheKnot.com or WeddingChannel.com; however, keep in mind that you could get bombarded by e-mails from their advertisers. You have to decide if daily deleting is worth it to you.)

Table seating card: Instead of paying a bundle to have everyone's name printed or calligraphed onto cards, try using clear labels and printing them out at home through a laser printer or ink jet. Then you can affix the labels onto cards. If there are last-minute cancellations and you have to switch tables, you won't encounter a last-minute panic, and you'll save on printing costs. We had our printer design nice business-size cards with a red Golden Gate Bridge icon at the top. Then, two nights before the wedding, we printed clear labels and affixed them to the cards, which we numbered with the final seating arrangements. They looked absolutely beautiful, and unless you inspected the cards closely, you couldn't even tell that we had used clear labels instead of printing directly on the cards.

> ## Who knew?
>
> Because many of your guests are likely to be couples, you can cut costs on your wedding favors by attaching them to seating cards. Count how many couples will be attending, and allot only one favor per couple. Then attach the couple's seating card to the gift they will share. We taped our seating cards to CDs, which we gave away as favors, and it worked out perfectly.

Thank-you notes: Of course, thank-you notes are essential and should be absolutely beautiful, but they don't need to be wedding-specific, and you needn't have them special-order printed. We had some beautiful one-sided cards printed up that simply said "Nina & Michael" on the top. We used them for thank-you notes for the wedding, but we also use them now as thank-you notes for dinner parties, overnight stays at a friend's place, or a thoughtful gift.

You can find tasteful cards in boxes of twenty-four or more at cost-friendly outposts like Office Depot for prices less than $6 a box. Remember: Since you're writing thank-you notes to some couples, you won't even need as many as the total number of guests. Even if you account for additional gifts from your engagement party or shower, these cards should only cost a total of about $25 for about 100 cards.

Who Knew?

When selecting your thank-you notecards, aim small. That way you won't find yourself struggling to fill a huge page with pat clichés.

Dear Great-Aunt Silvie,
The carving knife you gave us completely sets the tone for our new, shared kitchen. We will treasure it forever, and think of you every single time we use it, whether for turkey, brisket, or chicken. There is no other item on our registry we wanted more.
Merci!

The Beauty of Bundling Orders

*A*s you begin to plan your wedding stationery package, deciding what's in and what's out, what's necessary and what's not, it's wise to bundle everything you'll want to order at once to cut down costs.

Printing everything at once allows a stationery store to cut all the components (invitation, RSVP, table card, and so on) out of one big sheet of paper. If you were to order invitations and then table cards separately, both requiring the same stock of paper and the same font, they would have to reset the machines and your costs would rise. Plan ahead at the outset and decide which elements you'd like in your paper package. When we ordered our invitations, we also printed thank-you notes, envelopes, RSVP cards, table cards, and an information sheet.

One Plus One Equals . . . One

*A*re you inviting two roommates or an entire family to your wedding? There's no need to send more than one invitation to one address. When determining how many invitations you plan to order, think through how many people actually need their own invitations. One bridal consultant recounts mistakenly leading a client to order one invitation for each person on the guest list, which amounted to 600 total. The printer "laughed all the way to the bank," she says ruefully. "We were going to wallpaper a room with the leftover invitations, thank-you cards, response cards, and reception cards." She would have been far better off taking some time to count up how many couples the bride and groom were intending to invite to cut down on the number of invitations.

While bundling invitations may be wise financially, it can also have the unintended effect of sending ambiguous sexual signals. We sent one invitation to our friends Josh and Matthew, two graduate students who live together in Brooklyn. Michael's mother called us one evening with a gentle inquiry about Josh's "newfound" sexual orientation. Both of our parents had assumed that the two roommates were an item because we packaged them together. Oops!

If you do choose to send two roommates one invitation, be sure to address it to both roommates clearly on the outer envelope and enclose enough RSVP cards for each individual, in case one person can come and the other cannot.

Different Printing Processes

*B*efore you head to a stationery shop and dive into forty-pound binders of invitation options, you should educate yourself about the different printing processes. That way, when you walk in to a chic shop and the helmet-haired proprietress barks out, "Engraved or letterpress?" as her greeting, you'll be able to wave your finger and toss back, "We're thinking thermography, my friend."

Unless you're a stationery junkie or a graphic designer, this terminology will all be new to you. That's fine. Here's your EZ Invite Printing Guide to bone up on the basics (from most to least expensive):

Letterpress: This newly trendy but old-fashioned process for printing wedding invitations requires a labor-intensive set of actions involving inking an image to produce an impression that is stamped by metal plates into paper. The effect? Imprinted characters. Run your finger

Who Knew?

Cheree Berry, an independent stationer in New York City who works by day as a graphic designer at Kate Spade, suggests cutting down the cost of letterpress by using one color ink. Each color you choose requires a new plate.

over the surface and you'll feel the grooves of the printed characters. Letterpress allows you more options with your paper choices, choosing thicker stock and allowing greater nuance of your colors. The effect is stunning and retro (think Kate Spade). But the cost can be just as stunning as the visual effect. We chose it as one of the few areas in which to splurge, because as magazine editors and publication junkies, text was critical to us for setting the tone.

Engraving: In this posh process, characters appear slightly raised on the front side of the paper, producing the sharpest image of any method. This is one of the priciest printing processes, mostly because of the special equipment it requires.

Thermography: For folks enamored with engraving but less pleased with the price, thermography is a popular option. It's sort of a sneaky pseudo-engraving, in that the process combines ink and powder to create letters that pop from the page. The only noticeable difference from the pricier version? The text can be a bit shinier, and the back of the invitation gives itself away because there's no dent from the raised letters.

Who Knew?

Why not get one engraved invite as a memento for yourself and then have the rest of your invitations printed using thermography? You could save hundreds of dollars.

Offset: Your classic "flat" printing used for magazines, found at every copy shop across the country and on fliers, stickers, and company letterhead. Because of the simplicity, this can be one of your cheaper options.

Who Knew?

If your budget requires offset printing, but you have designs on dressing it up, why not glam up your graphics with bold colors? Using distinctive hues can let you get away with cutting costs in your printing budget. Remember, however, that colored ink can be more expensive than black ink, so be sure to ask. Using colored ink in flat-based printing still might work out to be less than using black ink for a pricier process.

Ink jet: Your tried-and-true, faithful dinosaur of a printer that's collecting dust next to your computer. It's not raised; it's not imprinted. It's as simple as they come—ink on paper. But even simple flat printing at home can be easily dressed up with cool fonts and chic paper colors.

For those who opt to save on printing costs, this can be a great option for printing programs or simple invitations.

What a Difference a Printing Process Makes

It's certainly helpful to know your terms, but how much can you save by choosing one printing process over another? As a sample, Union Street Papery in San Francisco allowed us to comparison-shop, printing the same invitation a variety of ways. For twenty-five invitations, here's the price difference they quoted:

ENGRAVING: $264
LETTERPRESS: $217
THERMOGRAPHY: $124
INK JET: $12.50

Paper Primer

Whether you will choose to do the designing yourself or drop off the assignment at your local shop, knowing your paper lingo can help you save money. There are three basic kinds of paper stock that you should learn about before even embarking on your invitation extravaganza.

Cover stock: You may recognize this option from products like brochures or menus. This is one of the most popular options for wedding invitations.

Index-card stock: Thicker than cover stock, this paper proba-

Who Knew?

If you're in the market for supremely cheap, flat printing, your best bet is to locate a discount printer who does bulk work or corporate work. Here's how it works: You provide the paper, design your invite yourself on your computer, and send it to the printer as a PDF file. They take care of the rest. One outfit quoted a price of $32 for 100 invites. That's about the same as a printer cartridge for your ink jet at home.

bly won't work in your average printer, as it may be too heavy. While many people find it to be too thick for their invitations, Michael and I loved the thickest stock.

Vellum: The surface on this super-thin, popular, filmy paper is a little rough. Since vellum is see-through, it works well for layering. While it's a hit with wedding invitations, vellum works best in conjunction with other types of paper as part of a larger package.

Shred Your Invitation Printing Costs

Whatever the printing option or paper stock you settle on, you can always enhance your final product yourself with easy, innovative tweaks. Why not . . .

• **Line your own envelopes with a stand-out color.** Buy paper in your favorite color. National stores like Paper Source sell an easy template for $9.50, which includes all the supplies you'll need to cut the paper to the right size and slide it into the envelope neatly.

• **Get the most mileage out of any custom-designed logo.** We had our printer do an illustration of the Golden Gate Bridge, since we were getting married across the bridge in Marin County. We saved the PDF file proofs on our computer and used them as a resource to design the jackets of CDs that we gave as wedding favors. It became our unifying graphic theme for the wedding, and we used it wherever we could—from the favors to the table cards.

• **Add pretty detailing to no-frills invites.** If you've purchased basic flat-based or offset-printed invitations, try embellishing them with a tied-on ribbon. Alternatively, use glued beads to dot your i's or to embellish any other characters that separate blocks of text.

• **Ditch ordering extras like tissue, vellum, and overlay, and take on the easy task yourself.** Tissues you order through the printer could cost you about $.50 a sheet. Forget it. Head to the architectural-supplies section of your local office store like Office Depot, where you can pick up a fifty-sheet pad of 8½-by-11-inch vellum for about $5. If you don't trust your own shaky hand, Kinko's can cut it down for you for $5, making your total cost $10. That could easily save you $40 on your invitations.

Who Knew?

Just like heavy coats or ripe plums, invitations have their peak season when it's best to order to get the lowest prices for the highest-quality products. Most stationery catalogs debut in January. That means the fresh, new designs carry with them fresh, new (aka higher) prices. This is one time when waiting until the new year to make a purchase won't help you save on after-Christmas sales. Don't delay in ordering your invites. Put in your order before the new year and cash in on last year's equally eye-catching models.

Vetting Vendors

*W*hether your budget is more Kmart or Kate Spade, Target or Tiffany, you can still shoot for high design. The key to wedding preparations, as well as anything shopping-related, is to do comparative research. Sure, you might like a pair of black boots Nordstrom, but who's to say they might not have a version that's equally as cute at Nine West? In order to get the ball rolling, here is a sample price comparison of one order done a number of different ways. Whatever you desire, you'll find printing options for all sorts of price points.

The Product: 100 Formal Triple-Panel Ecru Cards and Envelopes

SHOP #1: CRANE'S (WWW.CRANE.COM)

Method 1: engraving
Price: $512 ($330 for invites and $182 for outer envelopes)
Method 2: thermography
Price: $297 ($181 for invites and $116 for outer envelopes)

SHOP #2: ENCORE STUDIOS (AVAILABLE AT WWW.MYGATSBY.COM)

Method: thermographed on fine, heavy paper with embossed pearl border
Price: $216 (for invites and blank envelopes)

SHOP #3: CARLSON CRAFT (WWW.CARLSONCRAFT.COM)

Method: flat
Price: $102.40 ($69 for invites and $33.40 for printed envelopes)

SHOP #4: OFFICE DEPOT (WWW.OFFICEDEPOT.COM)
Method: flat (like the "business announcements" they often print)
Price: $91 ($66 for invites and $25 for printed outer envelopes)

Decoding Price Differences

What does all that mean?

• Even if you splurge at the upmarket Crane's, you can slash more than $40 from your invite budget just by opting for thermography instead of engraving. And as we've learned above, it's hard to even tell the difference between the two processes.

Who Knew?

However many people you plan to invite, allot for an additional twenty-five invitations. If you end up resorting to inviting the C-list and coming up short on invites, you'll need to put in a minimum order, which can be as much as fifty invitations. You could potentially save hundreds of dollars in the long run by slightly padding your order at the outset. That's because small print runs can be more expensive per invite than larger ones.

• Avoiding the classic wedding shops like Crane's can save you serious cash. They may be the industry standard for invites, but the same product can cost you more than 25 percent less at an online store. One great website where you can find beautiful mail-order invitations is www.reavesengraving.com.

• If you're fine with going flat, head to Office Depot, where their primary focus isn't doing All Things Wedding ($$). Sure, it might not have cachet, but you'll walk out with more cash in your pocket to allocate elsewhere.

Hidden Cost:
Proofs

You've decided on the paper you'd like, you've found the font of your dreams, you've put in your order, and you've picked up some skills with the calligraphy pen. You're set, right? Not just yet. When you shop around for invitation vendors, be sure to ask if the folks you're hiring are factoring in prices for proofs. You might find yourself unpleasantly surprised by their answer. Stationery stores sometimes charge between $7 an item and $30 total to let you look over the work before it goes to press.

Don't fool yourself and put too much faith in the spelling skills of others, especially if you have a last name like mine (*Willdorf—that's two Ls*). Peeking at proofs is absolutely worth it. The key is to negotiate with the vendor to have them reduce or eliminate the fee. If you are dealing with a smaller, independent shop, ask at the beginning if they'll throw in the proof for free. If you are bundling your purchases and putting in a big order, remind them of that. If they are unwilling to let you see the hard-copy proof for free, find out if they will send you a PDF file. The folks we hired, SoHo Letterpress, e-mailed us a file that we were able to look at on-screen. It's really no extra work for them, so don't succumb to an unnecessary added charge.

DIY Invites: Could Doing It Yourself Do You In?

here are some noble women in this world who aren't afraid of craft glue and who take on projects involving paper cutters, fine ribbon, and rhinestones with a twinkle in their eye and an agile touch. My friend Megan, who works, appropriately, at *Martha Stewart Living Magazine,* is precisely one of those women. So when confronted with the project of creating wedding invitations, doing it herself was the obvious, most appealing choice for her. She would be able to make exactly what she wanted for a price that she could contain.

In a lucky stroke, Megan and I got engaged within a month of each other, and our weddings were within two months of each other's, so our planning processes were wonderfully simultaneous. Like new moms, we'd call the other with excitement or angst to check in, to swap strategies, and simply to ask: "Wait a minute, *is this normal?*"

One day I called her while she was in mid–Wedding Invite Mode. "I'm in craft hell!" she moaned. "You don't even want to know. . . ." She muttered something about a glue mishap, wondering if a rhinestone would still adhere after it had gone through the mail, and some obscure printing process. I left her to it.

About a month later, her invitation arrived in the mail. It was an exquisitely crafted two-sheet affair with the vellum invitation superimposed on a vintage-style photo of a journal opened to a personal entry. I was floored. It was beautiful, personal, and fine. (The rhinestone, thankfully, had not moved from the top of the invitation.) How had she done this?

You could chalk it up to blood, sweat, and tears. "It's incredibly labor-intensive," says Claudia Hanlin of New York City's Wedding Library, a company that compiles research on vendors for brides in addition to offering wedding-planning services. "There's a reason you don't see stationers running around in Mercedes XLs."

But brides aren't in this for the cold, hard cash. In fact, in the effort to save some, the craftiest among us might be inclined to follow my friend's lead and pave their own way with their super-chic printing. If you're up for the task, it's important to know that going DIY isn't always cheaper. You still need to make wise choices in your quest to squeeze the most out of your budget. After spending $150 on stock paper and $150 for duplication at a printing shop, as well as countless hours of time, it's likely you're not going to be paying less than you would to farm out the labor. That's why going DIY requires some creative budgeting.

Who Knew?

Doing it yourself doesn't mean you must resign yourself to old-school Print Shop, Times Roman, and a single cream sheet of paper run off your laser printer. It's possible to make your own letterpress invitations. At outfits like the San Francisco Center for the Book, for example, you can take classes that will instruct you in the art form. Three required classes cost a few hundred dollars. Then you'll be set to rent their sturdy machines for an hourly fee. All told, you can save hundreds of dollars—and pick up a new hobby. Call around in your town to see if your local university or art school offers a similar course of instruction. Best of all, you'll not only be paying to print your wedding invitations, you'll be picking up a new skill that you can use later. *Baby shower invites, anyone?*

Budget-Minded DIY Do's and Don'ts

1. **Don't purchase an invite kit unless it's a sure thing.** Reni Schriek of TruSo Designs had a client who made the mistake of ordering a half-baked kit off of Ebay. The invitations ended up looking like your standard Powerpoint presentation. Alternatively, Paper Source has a great selection of DIY kits, which cost between $125 and $250 per 100 invites. Here's how they work: You print info on a small sheet and then glue it onto a precut

backing card, then polish them off with decorative wrap or ribbon and voila! Welcome to my wedding . . .

2. **Do avoid precut pieces of paper.** They will always be more expensive than oversized sheets of heavy card stock. How hard is cutting something to size, anyway? Your best option will be to use a paper cutter at your local Kinko's, but an Exacto knife and a steady hand could also work.

3. **Do go all the way.** Purchase whatever paper you use at discount stores like PaperDirect or Party City. The savings will be significant. While print shops can charge $.08 to $.10 a sheet for ivory cover-stock sheets, office-supply stores often sell them in packs of 250 for as little as $10 total. Don't be half-hearted about your savings.

4. **Do test, test, test.** Chances are your trials will include many errors. Testing more at the beginning will actually cut down costs in the end, so you're not accidentally wasting

Wedding Chic
Word to the Wise

Here's one DIY unnecessary extra: a Xyron machine. This gadget, which costs about $40, applies an even layer of adhesive as a way to laminate. Honestly, will anyone really be focusing on the teensy lumps, if there even are any? This is one time when it's worth it to take a breath . . . and let it go.

Who Knew?

Making invitations doesn't have to be a boring solo affair, with you sitting cross-legged in the living room, covered in Elmer's glue. Arrange a girls' getaway weekend with your closest pals whom you never get to see. Then glue, stick, address, collate, *and* catch up to your heart's content.

supplies after overlooking a potential problem. Megan tested every stage along the way when making her invitations, all the way up to sending one to herself in the mail to make sure it held up.

5. **Don't waste money matching paper colors to a photograph.** Be warned that colors change from your computer to the page. If you spend hours—and half your budget—on the perfect hue for the background, the photo may surprise you. Print out your image *first*—before painstakingly selecting paper.

Your Invitation-Crafting Supply Kit

aking your own invites could be a fun project as well as a money saver—but only if you know how to make wise buys. Here are the basic supplies you'll need to get started with a simple, elegant invitation:

Paper and envelopes made of quality stock (it's best to buy in bulk)
Ruler
Paper cutter
Glue stick
Craft glue

Hole punch
Vellum and vellum tape
Fun extras, like rhinestones, charms, and ribbon

Big-Store, Low-Budget Invite Ideas

There is, of course, a middle ground between hiring someone to take over the whole invitation process, from conception to calligraphy, and taking on every ounce of the project so much so that you're covered in cuts and glue for months. There is a zone of pseudo-DIY. Incorporate some of the ease of farming out labor with the glory of getting your hands dirty.

- **Crane's Imprintables.** Crane's has started a new line of printer-compatible cards, in sets of 10 cards and lined envelopes, for under $15. They're pretty, and pretty easy to use.

- **Office Depot's wedding kit,** including 25 invites with envelopes and notecards with envelopes for about $30. This set isn't about high gloss and high glamour, but the low price makes it worth a look.

Worthy Websites

Check out these online spots for nice discounts on your wedding invitations. (Beware, however, that some don't accept returns, and you should insist on having a sample sheet of paper sent to you before placing any kind of order.)

www.einvite.com
www.mygatsby.com
www.paper-source.com
www.invitationsbykarina.com

Address Yourself Properly

hether you've chosen to do everything yourself, have your invitations printed, or take on part of the task and farm out the rest, and whether you've chosen letterpress on index-card stock, engraving on cover stock, or simply flat-press on vellum for everything, there's one crucial detail that everyone must attend to before these puppies are signed, sealed, and delivered. In fact, some might say that the most important part still awaits: addressing the invitations.

I recently attended an event at the Vera Wang boutique on Madison Avenue in New York City, hosted by *Martha Stewart Weddings* magazine. Well-maintained Manhattan brides alighted up the staircase, swilling champagne, nibbling on chocolate cake (*not too much, though!*), and running their French-manicured fingertips over lacy gowns. Representing the invitation industry was one company that bills itself as the wedding calligrapher for those in the "right" circles. These folks are discreet; and they don't quote a price until they've surveyed the whole situation—and the size of your ring. But to get a sense for how much a hand-calligraphed invitation could cost, low-end prices start at $1 a line, per envelope. For at least three lines on 100 invitations, that adds up to . . . *way* too much.

Certainly, it is important that your wedding invitations are not addressed in the same chicken scratch you use to send in your electricity bill. That said, spending hundreds of dollars to have invitations addressed is certainly an unnecessary extra for one main reason: People rip open wedding invitations with excitement, passing by their names while they head for the more important real estate—what's *inside*. If you choose to splurge on hand-calligraphed addresses, you're not going to get that much bang for your buck. It's best to devote your dollars elsewhere and consider these attractive alternatives:

• **Write them yourself.** As I've grown older, my handwriting gets more and more illegible. I think I was sick the day in grade school when they impressed the idea that loopy, neat letters were best, and now I covet coworkers' penmanship on office birthday cards. If you attended class that day, by all means spend a few evenings at home with a fresh roller-ball pen and do it yourself.

• **Try your hand at DIY calligraphy.** If you like the look of calligraphy but don't want to spend the money to hire someone to do it for you, try teaching yourself. Purchase a kit that comes with sharp pens and a letter-by-letter guide, and practice away. Give yourself a few months to hone your craft. Make sure you have ample extra envelopes if you're still a super-novice when it comes time to actually put the pen to real paper. Take this as another opportunity to teach yourself a valuable skill.

• **Consider printing your envelopes at home.** After trolling around freeware sites for the perfect elegant font (you can find websites with free fonts to share by simply doing a Google search for "freeware fonts"), we decided that this was the best option for us. If it makes you nervous to print directly onto your envelopes (we practiced, and practiced, before running the real deal through the printer), try printing on clear mailing labels, which you can then adhere to the envelopes. The end result won't be as pretty, but your invitations will be more likely to come out mistake-free.

• **Ask Grandma.** She's incredibly excited about the wedding. She's always been trying to impress upon you the importance of good penmanship. And frankly, you've never seen such perfect script as hers. Why not squeeze some labor out of the older generation?

Sending: The Dollars and Sense of Postage

One of the wisest things you can do at the beginning of the invitation-planning process is select your paper size and weight wisely. Why? Because it could drastically affect your postage costs. The U.S. Postal Service charges 37 cents for an envelope, up to one ounce, that ranges in size from 3½ by 5 to 6⅛ by 11½ inches. The big surprise to many brides is that even if your envelope is too small, the price will go up; the surcharge on smaller or larger cards is $.12 per card. Plan to use cardstock in the USPS-friendly range, and you will be able to use regular stamps.

Who Knew?

Have some fun with your stamp selection. Why not put Audrey Hepburn on the outside and Cary Grant on the inner envelope or RSVP cards? Get creative. Using "Love" is so obvious!

The Contract Basics

any invitation print shops don't draft contracts, but it can be helpful to get a few matters in writing before placing your order. Be sure to have these points written in ink:

• The specifics of your order (quantity, price, and paper stock).

• The due date.

• Any extra fees that will be required (such as for proofs).

• The deposit amount, and when it is due.

• If there is a "price-escalation" clause, which factors in flexibility for additional, unforeseen expenses, be sure it is capped at no higher than 15 percent.

• The company's refund policy.

The Bottom Line

• Finalize who makes the cut on your guest list (a smaller list will be friendlier to your budget).

• Pare down the number of items (beyond invites) that you plan on having printed, such as reception cards and ceremony programs.

• Bundle orders for the best prices.

- Consider cost-effective printing processes and card stock to save extra money.

- Search out savings-friendly vendors.

- Don't rule out doing it yourself.

- Open your eyes to little creative ways to shave costs.

- Trim your postage costs by choosing cost-friendly paper sizes and weights.

3 · The Venue:

Place Yourself in the Right Price Range from the Beginning

our local barbeque joint, or your city's lush botanical gardens? Poolside, or at a historic mansion? The middle of a shopping mall on a buzzing Saturday afternoon, or an abandoned hillside? Where you choose to have your wedding truly determines its general feeling and sensibility. And the range of possibilities is enormous—from spots decorated with Vegas-y flashing lights to more dimly lit affairs, from secluded areas to mass wedding emporiums where you are Wedding #3 of the day, down the hall and third room on the left.

Your options are almost endless when it comes to choosing both where you would like to say "I do" and where you'll watch your guests do the funky chicken in celebration afterward. But though the world might be your oyster, there are only so many pearls to be found in the wild world of weddings.

Wherever you decide to hold your wedding, there's no reason that you can't keep your budget under control. All you have to do is educate yourself about the fine print, the variety of options available, and what they each entail. Armed with the information in this chapter, making a wise choice for *your* wedding venue will be as easy as that stroll down the aisle you're about to take.

Choose Your City Wisely

One of the most important ways you can keep your wedding costs down is by being thoughtful about the place where you'll be making the transition from Miss to Missus. Hours after getting engaged, Michael and I were already facing one of the largest decisions we had to make, as our parents excitedly peppered us with questions: *Who? Where? When? How? Where? Where? Where?* (The only thing they didn't ask was *Why?*)

I grew up in San Francisco, and my family still lives there. One of the first things that Michael and I talked about when we met in Boston was the Bay Area, as both his parents were raised in the greater Bay Area, and most of his family still lives there as well. It seemed the obvious choice to get married somewhere on the Left Coast.

However, we live in New York, as do most of our friends. Requiring all of our pals to pay for a cross-country flight, hotel, and car rental seemed like it would necessarily limit the attendance of many people whom we really cared about. Would having our wedding in San Francisco mean that the event would be 80 percent parents and their local friends, and 20 percent our guests? Would having it across the country limit the amount of control we would have about details that were meaningful to us?

Ultimately, we did opt to have the wedding in San Francisco, for two major reasons: time and money. Because both of us have full-time, demanding jobs, there was certainly something nice about being able to enlist the help of my parents, who could scout things out for us and report back, constantly e-mailing digital photos and essential information. Despite the fact that San Francisco is not exactly a cheap town, we felt we would get significantly more for our money there than in New York City, where $22,000, about the national average cost of a wedding, gets you take-out Chinese food and a movie ticket. We certainly could have done it in New York, but it wouldn't have been the event we wanted. Instead, while sitting down and contemplating the amount of money we had to spend on a wedding, we decided we could more closely approximate the elegant affair we wanted by hightailing it out of town. So we made the choice to maximize our budget by heading West.

Similarly, it may be worth it to head for the hills for your wedding. Small-town prices can have a big impact on your bridal bottom line, from venue-rental prices to catering costs. Even the region of the country where you get married can significantly affect your final price. While the average price of an American wedding is over $22,000 according to the Condé Nast Bridal Infobank, a wedding costs more than $11,000 *over* the national average for folks in the New York metropolitan area, where the average wedding costs $33,424. Meanwhile, the Infobank reports that Southern brides shave about $4,000 off the national average, paying an average of $18,624, and folks in the West and Northwest save more than $1,000, paying an average of $21,156. (The Northeast is the second most expensive region, clocking in at $29,788 for average wedding costs.) This was all the more reason for us to leave New York City.

The Beauty of the Destination Wedding

If you're the type who scours the Sunday travel section for deals and jets off on a whim—or if your family is so huge that the reality of planning your wedding will involve decades of debt in order to accommodate everyone—you might be a prime candidate for a destination wedding. Having your nuptials in Nevis can seem extravagant at the outset, but it will carry the best wedding gift of all: the beauty of not needing to invite everyone and their mother. A destination wedding will require your penny-pinching pals to head halfway around the world and hop a twelve-seater propeller plane to a tropical island. So only the truest friends—the ones you absolutely want there—will come, allowing you to really maximize your dollars. Simply say, "Yeah, we're having a small event on a secluded beach in Portugal," and see how fast coworkers squelch the uncouth impulse to assume they're invited.

Venue Types from A to Z

*O*nce you've figured out the general neck of the woods where you plan to tie the knot, it's time to home in on some location options. Think broadly. Instead of just heading to the local hotel and scoping out the generic banquet room (*Great carpet! Cool overhead projector!*), start brainstorming about alternative ideas, which abound all over the country. Here is a sampling of venues to get the mental wheels turning:

Arboretum
Aquarium
Art gallery
Army base (no joke . . . Sir!)
Backyard
Beach
Community center
Greenhouse
Hotel
Las Vegas
Library
Museum
Park
Private club
Restaurant
Theater
University
Zoo

Who Knew?

Why not call a movie-location scout? Their stock and trade is to find the holy grail—abandoned, beautiful, low-budget locations. Offer to pay them a small fee for their expertise.

With each type of venue comes a whole new set of rules: The university has a 10:00 p.m. curfew; the hotel mandates that you use its pricey in-house caterer; the beach will require you to rent tents in case of rain. What may seem like the perfect space at first glance often has unexpected drawbacks. And vendors aren't likely to volunteer specific information on the additional surcharges upon first meeting you. For example, a beautiful white-washed art gallery may seem exquisite at first, but there are many angles to consider.

Here's what the location manager sees: a flush taker for a prime Saturday night mid-summer.

Here's what you see: a chic minimalist space in primo territory in the center of town.

Here's what no one sees—yet: thousands of extra dollars on your floral budget to soften the starkness. Major rental fees to bring in everything you need, from chairs to pedestals for flowers.

For example, I got married at a yacht club in Tiburon, California. I wasn't able to inspect the space, because I was in New York when we had to book our venue. However, my parents promised to be our eyes and ears, and my two sisters also went along for the ride. The

beauty of a yacht club is that it's right on the water, and this particular spot had a gorgeous, sparkling view of the San Francisco Bay, along with a jagged slice of the breathtaking California coastline. The downside to yacht clubs is that they flaunt their flags from various races, which hang down from the ceiling. While I love the sea, yachting flags weren't exactly the aesthetic I'd envisioned at my wedding.

Yet the venue coordinator tossed off the question about whether or not the flags could be taken down. "No problem!" she said with a swift nod of her head. (Learn to be skeptical of that phrase when you're planning a wedding; even if things aren't a problem, they can be problematic financially.) What she didn't volunteer quite so readily was the fact that "flag removal" showed up on the final bill, with a price tag of $250. And the beautiful tulle and lights that she had touted in photos of previous weddings tacked an additional $450 on to the bill. By that time, however, we had already signed a contract, and taking down the nautical flags was worth any price. *Two-hundred and fifty dollars? Fine . . . Just make them go away!* But knowing in advance to ask every single question that pops up—along with forcing vendors to elaborate on any "no problem!" that they nonchalantly offer—will set you up to be the most informed wedding consumer possible. Remember, there's no such thing as a dumb question, especially when it comes to your wedding.

If you know which questions to ask when you're shopping around, you'll be able to get the most complete prices to compare. That way, the beautiful wedding you envision won't get the best of you when unknown surcharges are added secretly at the last minute.

Each venue can have its own pluses and minuses, so to give you a sense of the kinds of questions you'll want to ask when scoping out potential spots, think about the following:

• **Hotels.** Though the original venue rental price may be less, extra tacked-on charges at hotels add up fast, making your total bill higher than at almost every other type of venue. Why? On your final bill, be prepared to find a banquet service charge, a banquet room rental charge (if you don't meet the required minimums for food), beverage charges, a servers' service charge (separate from the gratuity), a bartender charge, alcohol charges, etc. Hotels also rarely let you BYOB, which could shave thousands of dollars off your bar bill. Ask from the outset about every single charge they bundle. Chair rentals? Required 25 percent service charge? An in-house caterer you must use? Fees to move chairs from one place to another? Don't underestimate the creativity a venue can use to add chargeable services.

- **Outdoor weddings, from your backyard to the beach.** It might seem romantic and low-key, but the backyard or outdoor wedding has sizable surcharges, starting with tent rentals. Also factor in rental charges for absolutely everything else, from chairs to tables to silverware to linens to glasses, and so on.

- **Restaurant.** Your favorite local restaurant can seem like the perfect place to get married. But beware that big events require much more than good food. You'll need to rent a dance floor (if you're so inclined), and figure out any amplification problems for your DJ or band. Amy Sohn, a columnist for *New York* magazine and the author of *Run Catch Kiss,* held her wedding at a restaurant called the Dream Away lodge, 2½ hours from New York City. "It was a very mellow, eclectic atmosphere, and as a result, our costs per head were much lower."

> ## Who Knew?
>
> Planning a super-small wedding? Rent out a luxurious suite in a fancy hotel for a few hundred dollars. You can invite your closest 25 friends, order room service, and begin celebrating. Best of all, nice hotels will have flowers there already—for no extra charge. As a wedding present, my friend Jeff supplied the room rental at a chic Boston hotel for his close friend's reception. They ordered room service and champagne—and had a truly fantastic time. Even if you don't have friends who are generous enough to foot part of the bill, a large room at a luxurious local hotel can be a wonderful setting for your intimate affair. Plus, then you don't have to rent the honeymoon suite in addition to your venue. You're already set, stumbling distance to bed!

Wise Questions to Ask

herever you decide to get married, try to negotiate cost-saving options in your contract. Here are some places to get started:

• **Request a BYOB situation.** Clubs and hotels that require you to imbibe from their own bottles do it for a reason: Selling booze is their bread and butter. Alternatively, if you buy in bulk at a local warehouse, you'll get substantially better prices, and you'll be able to return unopened bottles at the end of the night, which my friend Seth found to be an extremely beneficial move when he completely overestimated how much his family would drink at his wedding. Another friend, Meredith, bought all her alcohol at her local Sam's Club, paying only $500 total for 300 guests. "We overbought cups and stir sticks, but what we didn't use, we took back," she noted. (Check, however, to make sure a corkage fee—a per-bottle surcharge that restaurants charge you when you bring in your own bottles of wine or alcohol—isn't so high that it could counteract your sweet savings.)

• **Choose a caterer who includes china, tablecloths, and silverware in their price quotes, and stick with what they have.** Unless you're obsessed with tabletop designs, it's best to stick with what they've offered instead of dealing with hiring outside rental vendors and coordinating the whole shebang yourself. Do you really care about the difference between moss- or seafoam-colored tablecloths?

• **Be aggressive with your negotiations.** Don't just say OK when a vendor quotes a price. Instead, try a line like, "Well, I can't spend that, but I'd love to work with you. What can you do?" Pause. Wait. Let them respond. They may counter by asking what you can afford. Aim low, and you'll meet in reasonable territory. Consider it Negotiations 101, which you'll

Hidden Cost:
Extra Hours

You're in the moment, the flush is running high in your cheeks, everyone's dancing, and you're feeling the love. And the clock is ticking. When you signed the contract, you figured four hours would be plenty of time, but now the party isn't nearly over. Don't get stuck in that situation. Read the fine print well ahead of time and find out how much extra hours will cost you. Some venues charge as much as $1,000 an hour if you go over your allotted time, not to mention service charges. If you have your wedding at an off-time, perhaps negotiate an extra buffer hour as a "value added," an option or service which is included for free in lieu of discounts on the services you've already requested.

be able to perfect on your honeymoon when you're eyeing a silver necklace from a street vendor.

• **Find out if you will be charged per drink or per container.** If your preferred spot won't agree to your BYOB request, you'll still have some room to squeeze out some savings. Instead of letting a venue charge you for a full bottle if they've just cracked open a new one, ask to be charged per drink. That way, you won't pay at all for liquor that's left in the bottles.

Average Rental Costs

*I*n the abstract, it might not seem like such a big deal when a wedding venue coordinator tells you that you'll need to pay extra for tablecloths, silverware, table rentals, and glassware. "Sure, sure, no problem," you say. "Yada, yada yada." Then, the bill comes, your head starts swimming, and you madly compute how many months of salary your snazzy linen choice will set you back.

Every single one of these items (multiplied by a hundred or two hundred, depending on how large your list is) can send shockwaves through your system. But steel yourself. And bone up on the bridal basics so that you know ahead of time what things cost. You can budget accordingly, by making decisions about what you want to splurge on and where you can seamlessly save. To get a sense of costs, here are examples of average prices from the lower end of the scale, provided by Regal Rents, one of the country's major party-rental companies:

ITEM	PRICE	TOTAL (PER 100 GUESTS)
Basic white folding chairs	$2.20	$220
Tables, eight-person round	$8.20	$107
Linens (per table)	$11.60	$151
China (full set, including saucers)	$2.70	$270
Water glasses	$1.45	$145
Wineglasses	$1.45	$145
Silverware (stainless-steel)	$0.54 (five per guest)	$270

ITEM	PRICE	TOTAL (PER 100 GUESTS)
Napkins	$0.75	$75
Assembly fee for delivery, setup, and pickup		$55
Tents (figure 20 square feet/person)		$1,500 to $3,000
Grand total		$2,938 to $4,438

Who Knew?

Bundling the location of the ceremony and reception can be a beautiful thing in more ways than one. You'll significantly cut down on your rental costs, as you won't need to rent two separate sets of chairs. And your floral budget will also benefit, because you will be able to move arrangements from one end of the room to another when you move from ceremony to cocktail-fueled Macarena. Extra bonus: you'll also slash costs on your invitation budget, because you won't need separate ceremony and reception cards.

Yikes. Those prices can add up fast! If you choose a venue that doesn't include full place settings, tables, chairs, and glassware, you can figure on adding an additional $3,000 to $4,500 to your total venue budget. Remember, that is for the *low* end of the rental scale. These added charges provide some real incentive to opt for venues such as a restaurant or a private club, which include all dinnerware in the price. Your final toll will be far less than it would be if you rent out that blank space that would require you to furnish it from top to bottom.

Cost-Saving Venue Tips

hatever part of the country you choose to have your event in, it will pay to be an intrepid consumer. In the city, country, or suburbs, you can amass countless cost-saving strategies to shave your venue budget.

• **Join the club.** At sites like the American News Women's Club in Washington, D.C., members save $500 off rental costs, paying only $700 instead of the standard $1,200 for an evening rental. However, joining the club (which is open to all journalists, and not just women) is well worth it, as the annual dues are only $140 a year. Those in other fields should seek out similar industry deals. They exist everywhere! Similarly, churches and synagogues often have lower rental rates for members. Many major metropolitan areas have Junior Leagues and schools, as well as university clubs, with available spaces. Maybe it's time you found a little school spirit for that trusty alma mater. . . .

• **Think locally.** Some spots will give you a discount if you're a resident of the county. For example, the Brazilian Room in Berkeley's Tilden Park tacks on an additional $300 in rental costs for Sundays for anyone who resides outside of the county.

• **Befriend big government.** Presumably, you pay taxes. Here's your chance to reap the rewards. Call your local Parks and Recreation department and find out if it has venues that can be rented out for big events. My friends Emily and Dave held an elegant outdoor reception at a municipally owned mansion in Ann Arbor, Michigan. Every region has its own historic properties on well-maintained grounds. Best of all, public places run by city organizations have wallet-friendly prices.

• **Check the real estate listings.** That's right. If there's a mansion that's been on the market for months, call the broker and find out if the seller might be willing to rent it out for a night and squeeze a little cash out of their 10,000-square-foot wallet-drainer. It's not as unlikely as it sounds.

• **Use every available resource.** If you went to college, it's time to use that pride in your alma mater. If you are part of a professional organization, bone up on the secret handshake. Now is the time to call in all favors, because it can make a significant difference in the quality of your wedding. For example, I went to Columbia University. The religious center there, Earl Hall, has a special cut rate for people in the University community that ranges from as low as $650 for a

---

Wedding Chic Word to the Wise:
Don't Be a Double-Booked Bride

Before booking your venue, make sure to ask whether there are any other events scheduled for that day. You want to feel pampered, attended to, and special on your day, not simply Bride #2 (out of five). If possible, have it written into your contract that you won't be squashed with other events in the same space on that day.

weekday evening rental to $950 for a prime weekend time slot. That's pretty low for such a beautiful spot in the big city.

* **Befriend fellow couples.** It turns out that there was a wedding scheduled the night before ours at the yacht club where we were getting married. So when we arrived for the rehearsal the day before our big event, the place was all dressed up, with wedding tulle already hung. Instead of taking it down and putting it back up the next day—and charging us for "tulle installation"—we asked if it would be possible simply to share the cost with the couple getting married the day before us. Sure enough, it was no problem. When in doubt, ask for discounts wherever you can. The only way you can be *sure* you won't receive a discount is if you don't even bother to try getting one.

Timing Is Everything

O nce you've wisely settled on the where, it's equally important to figure out the second most fiscally important factor: the when. Sure, you may envision a lush spring wedding in Brooklyn's Botanic Gardens to savor the full bloom. Well, so do thousands of others, so be prepared to pay top dollar to see your fantasy come to fruition. Instead of simply following a rosy cliché, work backward and select your wedding date according to what will make the most sense financially.

* **Best seasons.** Summer and spring are the most popular seasons for weddings. Opting for fall or winter can save you serious cash. A bonus of having your wedding in the late fall is that you may be able to piggyback on the venue's holiday

decorations. Find out when your venue starts sprucing up for the holidays, and book your wedding for a date soon after that time. You'll cut down on your floral budget if you don't need to dress every inch of a drab space. Also, consider when your wedding city is going to be least appealing seasonally, and book it for just then! For example, a Southwest wedding in the summer will be piping hot and priced lower than a more seasonable fall or spring wedding. It's not like you're going to be having a relay race outside the wedding. There is such a thing as climate control. "We threw our wedding in the winter, March in Manhattan," notes Joel Stein, a writer in New York City. "The trick was, it looked really expensive but it wasn't, mostly because we took a weekend they couldn't fill."

Who Knew?

While holidays may seem like an appealing time to get hitched, the venue will tack on extra costs. Valentine's Day and Mother's Day will practically double your floral budget. And New Year's Eve will require a Bribe-al surcharge for labor, as most folks would rather be out toasting to the New Year themselves than topping off your guests' champagne glasses. In contrast, Super Bowl weekend can be a big money-saver if you and your intended (and your closest friends and family) aren't so into football. "Everyone is more flexible with their pricing on that day because they're not very busy," New York City wedding planner Elizabeth K. Allen told *The New York Times* in February 2004. "You'll have great availability in terms of locations, bands, and photographers."

- **Best months.** In general, the most budget-friendly months for weddings are November through March, as they fall into the wedding off-season. (The worst, busiest wedding months? In the Northeast, avoid May through September. In the South, avoid May or October.) Select any other month to get lower prices on rentals and vendors. Off-season discounts can come in various forms, whether it's a percentage off the total rental cost, or "value addeds"—extras included in the prices, like valet parking or free cleanup.

• **Best weeks.** Most folks don't think of the week between Christmas and New Year's as a wedding week, but that's precisely why it's a good time. People generally have time off work to travel, and prices are lower since it's a slow time for weddings. Avoid the week around the super-popular wedding date of Valentine's Day (except in Vegas; see more below), when Cupid's arrow strikes directly at your bank account.

• **Best days.** No surprise, but weekends are the most popular time for weddings. At many venues, even opting for a Friday-night affair rather than a Saturday event can save you 10 to 15 percent off your final bill. Scheduling on weekdays, particularly Mondays, will slash your savings even more. For example, a little birdie at New

York's posh Waldorf-Astoria dishes that the elite hotel has been known to cut bills by 10 to 20 percent for a weekday wedding. Not bad.

• **Best time of day.** An evening wedding is considered the classic, with dinner, dancing, and cocktails. However, if your budget will be super-stretched, shift the time of the event, and your prices will drop significantly. A late-afternoon wedding won't call for the same quantity of food. You can have substantial amounts of appetizers passed around or food stations, rather than a sit-down, four-course meal. Also, your booze budget will be far less, as people tend to drink less in

Wedding Chic Word to the Wise: Why Off-Times Can Be Off-Putting

While you are considering slick ways to slash your budget by timing it wisely, you should also be well aware that this should be done with the utmost consideration for your guests. Yes, you may save a few thousand dollars by having a Tuesday-morning wedding in a suburb of Sedona, Arizona, in the middle of July, but what will be the toll on your friends? A friend of mine recently attended a Sunday-evening wedding in New Jersey, grumbling all the way. "I think it would be sort of embarrassing," she told me. "Everyone would know you're having a cheap wedding." Sure, the bride may have saved a few bucks, but then the costs fall to the guests, and they pay the price the next day, staggering into work with a splitting postchampagne headache.

I was recently invited to a wedding on a Wednesday afternoon in New York City. Of course, the rental fees were significantly less for the wedding couple. But any guests who needed to be there would have to take time off work. So the couple saved . . . and the guests paid. It didn't exactly set the tone for a gracious event. Instead, think through your timing and only opt for an off-time if you think it won't put your guests out too much.

the afternoon than they do in the evening. Similarly, a lunchtime affair will be less expensive than dinner. Avoid, however, pushing an event up to the morning just to save a buck. It will lose a certain elegance if people have just rolled out of bed and are bleary-eyed as you're walking down the aisle. *Here comes the who?!*

The Difference a Day Makes

*I*n theory, choosing your wedding date by the calendar may seem all well and good, but how much of a difference can it actually make? Calls to some of the nation's most popular venues revealed some major, surprising savings tips. Share these only with your best friends!

- **House of Blues Foundation Room at Mandalay Bay in Las Vegas:** Having a wedding off-peak in February, August, or December will cost you a third less for your food and beverage minimum ($2,500) than if you opt for a super-peak month, such as March through June when the minimums shoot up as high as $7,500. (Peak months, July, September, October, and January, fall in the middle for their minimums, at $5,000.)

Who Knew?

While folks in the wedding industry may make you feel like a dope for planning your wedding *only* nine months in advance—*rush charges!*—you may be able to benefit from last-minute planning in your venue if you'd like to book a date within a few months. Why? If they have a free slot, it will be in their best interest to fill it. The same goes for a wedding on a weekday, when venues aren't as popular. Negotiate, negotiate, negotiate. Your lower rate will look better to them than the $0 they would get without you.

- **Seattle's Clise Mansion in Redmond's Marymoor Park:** This popular wedding venue costs 75 percent less to rent on weekday evenings from 6 p.m. to 10 p.m. than renting on peak summer weekends; the price literally ranges from $395 to $1,550.

- **Brooklyn's Botanic Gardens:** While having a wedding on a Saturday evening in the summer will set you back $4,000 in simple rental costs, this venue slashes rental prices by as much as about 70 percent for the off-peak times and seasons. For example, a daytime weekday wedding in December costs only $1,250. And don't worry, they heat the place.

- **Berkeley's Brazilian Room in Tilden Park:** Renting out this venue on a Sunday evening instead of a Friday evening costs about 20 percent less, $1,400 rather than $1,725. That even goes for a holiday weekend, when a Sunday can function as a pseudo-Saturday night.

The Down-Low on Deposits

hew. You've decided on the city where you want to get married, the date, and the place. Now it's time to start writing checks. Venue coordinators will urge you to put down as much as you can, as fast as you can. Don't worry; it's not necessary. You should never need to pay more than one-third of the full price up front for your facility fee deposit. (If the venue includes catering as well as rentals for chairs, linens, and all the finery, you can count on putting down a 50 percent deposit.) But most important, put your deposit on your credit card for safety's sake. That way, if there's a problem, your credit-card company may have you insured. (Check with your company to be sure.)

The World's Wedding Capital:
Viva Las Vegas!

hen I was in the hazy thick of planning our wedding, I began to envy anyone who had eloped. A former colleague from the *Boston Phoenix,* a weekly newspaper where Michael and I originally met, had jetted off to Las Vegas with his then-girlfriend in a rock-and-roll–fueled romantic frenzy, coming back with rings—and a great story.

Every year, Las Vegas lures similarly smitten couples, some in an impulsive 4 a.m. haze, and some meticulously planned and posh. Vegas weddings truly run the gamut from glitzy and glamorous to gauche. In fact, it's the kind of town where a stroll along the strip will ensure you at least one run-in with a trashed bachelorette wearing a beat-up white ribbed tank top and a veil, and slinging a Budweiser. From the high to the low, here's what you want to know about getting hitched in Sin City:

* **It's not as cheap as you might think.** Vegas has a rep of offering $1.99 buffets and $99 hotel suites to the low rollers among us. It's not necessarily so. Having a Vegas banquet wedding can set you back as much as $70 a head at some spots. And it goes up—and up.

* **Planning in advance can be tricky.** Because Vegas is a popular spot for conventions, many large venues are hesitant to book banquet rooms more than ninety days in advance. Why? Although you might think your rental prices are steep, conventions rake in double the money. It's a high-stakes game. Use those odds to win. For precisely that reason, Vegas may be the perfect place to have a last-minute affair; when they know they won't be getting a convention, you'll be in

the prime position to lay down your cards. "In order for me to commit, I'll need you to do better on your prices."

• **Think February.** Who cares if it's technically winter. February in Vegas is one of the best times to get married, if only because of the fact that it's the slowest wedding month. Thanks to Valentine's Day, the shortest month of the year is a popular time to elope rather than have an elaborate affair. So you can be in prime position to negotiate rental prices, from your venue to your linens.

• **You can walk a well-worn trail.** Though they may not have stood the test of time, celebrity weddings have often taken place at one local Las Vegas spot, the Little Church of the West. Since 1942, this chapel, which claims to have housed more celebrity weddings than any other chapel in the world,

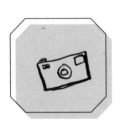

was the location for the nuptials of such folks as Zsa Zsa Gabor and George Saunders, and Richard Gere and Cindy Crawford. (Maybe they forgot the "as long as we both shall live" bit. . . .) The same aisle can be yours for as little as $199, plus a little something for the minister.

• **There is no end to how high you can go.** While we might be a budget-minded set, you can always dream about how the other half lives. In Vegas, the other half camps out at the Bellagio, where you can rent certain rooms that come with a minimum food charge of $10,000. (In a generous gesture, they don't charge for the room. Thanks!)

The Contract Basics

*B*efore signing, make sure the following points are addressed in your venue's contract:

* The date and time of the event.

* The name and contact info for the venue coordinator, the site address, and yourself.

* The hours you will have the venue.

* A specific outline of the fees (including a breakdown of costs).

* If there is a "price-escalation" clause, be sure it is capped at no more than 15 percent.

* The deposit due date, and the balance due date.

* The venue's cancellation and refund policy.

The Bottom Line

* Choose a financially friendly geographic location.

* Time your event wisely.

* Think broadly about the *type* of venue in which you could get married—and have your party.

* Consider all the extra (or included) costs that go hand in hand with the type of venue you're drawn to.

* Learn essential questions to ask before signing any contracts.

* Read all the fine print on the contract.

* Bone up on the average rental costs that you might need to
add on with certain types of venues.

* Home in on the best season, month, week, day, and times
to get good prices.

4 · The Threads:

Be Queen for a Day Without Getting Royally Ripped Off

*T*here's nothing more iconic about an American wedding than the vast lengths of smooth white fabric that make up a woman's wedding dress. It's one of the first things people ask about, and one of the elements of the wedding that can make the marriage-bound go truly bonkers. But it's important to remember that it's just that: a dress. And most likely, it's something you'll wear only once. Hopefully, that is.

My entire process of choosing a wedding dress was surprisingly free of angst. I had been prepared by so many friends for a moment I was supposed to experience. "You'll know it's the right one immediately. When you put on The Dress, you'll just burst into tears." It was hard for me to imagine. In truth, I hadn't known Michael was The One the minute I set eyes on him. We dated slowly, getting increasingly more serious. I don't even remember the first time we discussed moving in together—or getting married, for that matter. Our evolution was gradual, seamless. If that classic romantic pattern of Love at First Sight eluded me, why would things be any different with the dress?

But still, I set out like a good bride-to-be, with a list of local shops and two fashion-savvy friends in tow. From the beginning, I was absolutely set on not buying a "wedding dress." As someone interested in fashion and well-made garments, I felt that if I was going to splurge on a beautiful gown, I wanted it to be something I could possibly wear again, something that wasn't inextricably bound to be weddingware. I figured this would be my chance to buy a Valentino, a Norciso Rodriguez, an Ungaro. As long as I was prepared to spend a healthy sum of money, I wanted something that was high-quality, beautiful, unique—something free of cheesy material and cheap beads.

So I printed out a list of boutiques, put on my walking shoes, and hit the streets one Saturday morning. I started off at Barneys uptown, tried on some truly handsome frocks, and put one on hold, somewhat unconvinced if it was fancy enough. Then I started making my way downtown. From shop to shop, I began assembling some good ideas. At Nicole Miller, I tried on a strapless bridesmaid's dress that definitely could have worked—for only a few hundred dollars. It was a contender. In several more shops, I gathered a few additional options.

Then, by the end of the day, my pooped pals and I found ourselves at the last stop, an airy store in SoHo called Morgane Le Fay. On the racks, the long gowns in icy colors looked slim, simple, somewhat inconsequential. But when I put one of them on, my friends gasped. And I just didn't want to take it off. Ever.

But . . . I wasn't crying. There wasn't even a faint mist in my eyes. *Oh, oh.* Was this The One? I put it on hold and came back with my maid of honor, Sari. In a quick second, she confirmed my initial feeling. "This is Nina's wedding dress." My friend Emily came with me a few weeks later. "Good job!" she said simply. "Good job."

In one day, in a matter of hours, with a minimum of hassle, I had completed a time-honored ritual that usually involves an intricate dance, a coy jig of negotiations between saleswoman and bride-to-be, with one party teasing the other every step of the way. I didn't buy my dress at a boutique solely devoted to weddings, so I didn't have to do the dance—and I wanted it that way. Many people don't have it that easy. Others do want the Big White Dress, the Train, the Bodice, the Whole Nine Yards—and then some. The industry isn't necessarily set up in your favor. But it doesn't have to be that way.

One of my favorite articles ever written about the bridal dress industry is by Rebecca Mead, in the April 21, 2003, issue of *The New Yorker.* In a rare move, Mead actually reported on the psychology of the bridal salesperson, in addition to that of the consumer. "The romance that the retailer is most interested in promoting is not the one between bride and groom but that between bride and gown," she writes. Later, she observes, "Yet the structure of the bridal industry conspires to frustrate both bride and retailer; while they appear to be collaborating on a grand romantic project, their economic interests are very different. The bride is afraid that her naïveté will be exploited; the retailer is on guard against the bride who is shopping but isn't buying. A cycle of resentment can easily be established."

My goal is to demystify the process. Remember, it's just a dress. You're just a girl. This is just one day. Don't be scared by lingo, bizarre pricing strategies, folklore about how you're supposed to pass out, weeping, when you put on The Dress. No tears? No worries. Not every girl goes gaga in the same way.

Who Knew?

The average bride shops at between four and six stores before settling on The One.

What Drives Up the Price of That Pretty Frock?

A few thousand dollars for a dress may seem like an enormous sum of money. It is. But there are reasons beyond the W-word that maintain the high prices for bridalware. In fact, there are three main factors that combine to pump up the price of a wedding dress.

Luxe Labels

Those familiar with the fashion biz know that the label is the single most important factor in the price of a piece of clothing. When you pay through the nose for designer duds, you're paying for the name. A friend of mine used to work for a name-brand designer. "It would make me sick how much they'd mark up some of the clothes," she said. "We'd get a sample that cost ten dollars to make, and then we'd use the same fabric, the same cut, and charge insane amounts of money." Why? Take a look at the label. And when you're dealing with the bridal business, certain brands stick out as the go-to girls for wedding dresses: Vera Wang, Monique Lhuillier, Reem Acra, Carolina Herrera.

But while the national average for a wedding dress is still a steep $800, splurging on a wedding dress by one of these leading ladies can hike the price as high as $10,000 and up.

Fabulous Fabrics

Two similar dresses hang side by side. They're both by the same designer, and they're both from the same season. But one costs half the price. Why? The fabric. For example, switching from silk, satin, or taffeta to raw silk can drastically cut your dress budget, because raw silk is significantly less expensive yard for yard.

Indeed, here's one place where you can make a seamless cut to your budget by opting for a wallet-friendly fabric choice. Some of the most expensive fabrics for wedding gowns include silk and lace. How much of a difference can fabric make? Here's a sample of price differences in common wedding fabrics by the yard. (Figure that a simple dress with a small train will require eight to ten yards of fabric.)

TULLE:	$1.50 TO $4
CHIFFON:	$6.99 TO $29.99
ORGANZA:	$6.99 TO $59.99
POLY-SATIN:	$12.99 TO $18.99
SILK:	$12.99 TO $250
LACE:	$5 TO $600

Detailed Designs

Even if you opt for a silk organza A-line number by a no-name designer, you can still expect to pay top dollar if you have your sights set on lots of little touches like beadwork on the bodice or colored embroidery. Simple is always better on the budget, especially when it comes to your dress. And it's also often the most elegant and streamlined. Price hikes can happen in two ways: with the initial cost and for altering extras. So when trying to keep to the low end of the dress price scale, steer clear of these add-ons:

Who Knew?

You might find your $1,000 gown pricey. But in the grand scheme of things, that's chump change for some. One lady recently paid the loftiest price ever reported for a bridal gown in the United States. In the summer of 2003, an anonymous Syrian Jewish bride paid $300,000 for her wedding dress. And you thought your dress was pricey!

• **Detailing**, such as sequins, beadwork, or embroidery along the seams. When you get the dress altered, every single bead, thread, or sequin will need to be unattached and reattached with every snip and tuck.

• **Crinolines** under the dress. These puffy ballerina skirts can turn your fantasy frock into a nightmare nuisance if you need altering. That's because crinolines don't always fit through a sewing machine, so they require hand-hemming, which can cost as much as $30 to $40 per layer.

Beyond the initial price, a fancy lace gown with all the frilly fixins will cost you throughout the entire wedding process. Intricate designs will require more alterations, fancy fabrics are more expensive to press, and when the day is done, bulky inner architecture can hike up the price for simple dry cleaning to as much as $500.

The dress I finally settled on was a silk organza, spaghetti-strap one-layer affair. It wasn't technically a wedding dress, and so it didn't have a bodice, beading, or elaborate inner layers. But best of all, when I went to have some hors d'oeuvres that had been smeared onto a strap taken out after the affair was over, my dry-cleaning bill was a mere $30, an unheard-of sum when it comes to cleaning wedding clothes.

The same dry cleaner had its price list posted prominently on the wall. They listed the charge to clean Wedding Dresses as $400. While my dress was technically my wedding dress, it wasn't necessarily a Wedding Dress. And since I didn't waltz in announcing that I needed my wedding dress cleaned, they could easily have mistaken it for a run-of-the-mill gown. The move saved me hundreds of dollars—and my dress is still sparkling now. I didn't realize just how much I could save—and continue to save—when I originally bought the dress, just by choosing a gown that was simple in its construction.

Hidden Cost: Strapless Gowns

While it may cost the same at the outset, a strapless gown can tack on hundreds of extra dollars in the alteration process. The boning, the architecture of the dress that keeps you from flashing your guests, needs to be so precisely fitted that it may require one or two extra fittings. You don't want it so tight that you create a fleshy layer of overhang, and you don't want it so loose that you're tugging your way through the night.

Shopping Your Way to Wedding Dress Bliss

*L*ike anything else, there's a good time and many more not-as-good times to make a big-ticket purchase like your wedding dress. However, there are two different ideas about when the best times to buy are.

Twice yearly. At many small boutiques across the country, new stock comes in twice a year, in February and in August. If you head to a shop right before the new stock is due in, you can ensure great price reductions. Some stores will encourage you to avoid the August cut-rate prices if you're having a winter wedding, because the dresses will all be summer-style. But the fact remains: Chances are you aren't exactly going to be looking for a polar fleece–lined dress anyway. Don't worry about seasonality in a wedding dress. It's one of the few times when Labor Day doesn't really mark an uncrossable line in style choices. Post, pre, whatever. This is one time when light colors are appropriate wherever your event falls in the calendar.

Depending on the shelf life. At larger stores, owners don't have to be as dependent on new stock coming in to clear out the old; dresses are always moving, and dress trends aren't as important as they may be at an upscale boutique. For example, at the New York uber-outfitter Kleinfeld, seasonality isn't as important as it is at a smaller Madison Avenue boutique. Anything that hasn't sold for

> ## Who Knew?
>
> Just because a sample in a bridal boutique fits you perfectly doesn't mean that the dress that arrives with your name on it will fit exactly the same way. In stores, you try on a sample to choose a design you like, and to determine the general size, and then a dress is made for you (unless you manage to wrangle buying the sample itself; see below for more information). So expect some variation in fit.

two or three months is automatically discounted to be the same price as a sample, starting at 50 percent off.

My friend Emily put this kind of knowledge to great use at another big store, Barneys, when she was shopping for her wedding dress. When she saw a beautiful dress on a mannequin, she had a few questions for the saleswoman. How long has this been out? When did these dresses arrive? When are you expecting next season's dresses?

Emily was smart. She was gauging how much the store wanted—indeed, *needed*—to unload this mass of cream fabric to make room for the new. And sure enough, when she found out that the new dresses were due within a few weeks, she didn't hesitate to insist on an additional 25 percent off the sticker price. She got it.

Who Knew?

Sample gowns are often listed as size ten. But that's not necessarily the same size ten that we're all familiar with. In fact, in gown-speak, size ten is the same as size six or eight in regular clothing. If the price is low enough, and the dress isn't so monstrous that you're swimming in it, you might want to consider buying a sample that's too big and getting it altered. But pull out your calculator to determine if the savings on the original price will still outweigh what you'd spend on the alteration costs.

The Do's and Don'ts of Alterations

Congratulations! You've found the dress that makes your face flood. But it's only the beginning of the process. The sample gown you are currently swimming in is a little baggy under the arms, a little loose around the mid-section, and drooping onto the floor. "Don't worry! No problem!" the saleswoman coos, bustling around, tugging it behind you so that from the front all looks good. But while technically it may be no problem to take it in here, take it out there, you could encounter a big problem financially.

Many brides fall in love with a reasonably priced dress, only to get hemmed in to high alteration costs. When it comes to a gown, a simple nip and tuck is certainly something worth fretting about. Why? Alterations can add up fast. For example, here's just a sampling of some real prices charged by one upscale shop in New York City:

- Taking in both sides: $125

- Hems: $200 to $250

- Reducing or increasing dress size by two to three sizes: $700 to $800

You should note, however, that prices can vary dramatically. In fact, sometimes they're even related to the mood of the seamstress. "Some days I have a very good heart," notes the proprietress of the shop above, "and some days I give a major discount. I can get into that mood as well."

Instead of just praying that you hit a seamstress at the right time of the day, familiarize yourself with certain bridalware basics so that you can have a seamless alteration experience.

DO opt for machine-work over handwork. If you need your underthings hemmed, like a crinoline, don't bother spending double the price to have a little old lady work the machine, forking over as much as $40 a layer. Instead—especially when it comes to the underside of the garment—say yes to the sewing machine.

DON'T get bullied into paying "rush" charges for anything that takes more than three months. While many seamstresses might try to stress you out about how five months is "really tight," don't believe the high-cost hype when they tell you that it will require an extra sum to make your alterations. While one wedding seamstress may say she prefers having six months, another seamstress, who isn't specially involved in the wedding industry but is equally adept with a needle and thread, may scoff that all it really takes is a few weeks: "What are they doing? *Making* the dress?" If your seamstress starts talking about rush charges, that's your cue to rush out the door.

DO choose a nonwedding seamstress or even a tailor. While you might think you need a special wedding seamstress to attend to your wedding threads, a woman who doesn't specialize in All Things White can also probably do an equally stellar job—for a fairer price. The average charge for a wedding seamstress's work is about $550, and a regular seamstress can do the same job in a month (with all the fittings) for about $200. In the happy medium are some of the bridal superstores, like Kleinfeld, which charges a flat fee of about $400 for everything you need done. Even better, if you only need the most basic alterations (a shortened strap, for instance), take your wares to an expert tailor, who is likely to charge even less than a seamstress.

DON'T just automatically decide to have alterations done by the seamstress at a bridal salon. Bridal salons make big money on dress alterations. One salon in Austin, Texas, quotes a price of $200 for a simple hem alteration. Believe that you can—and should—do better.

DO ask ahead of time if alterations are included. I didn't realize ahead of time how good I had it when the salesgirl I worked with breezily added that alterations were included in the price. "Great," I said, lacing up my shoes absentmindedly. But I should have run over and kissed her. That little fact saved me as much as

$500—or more. Always ask, shop to shop, if the price includes alterations. Chances are, if you're heading to a bridal salon, they won't. In that case, get a written (signed) estimate of how much they expect the alterations to cost. Unfair bridal alteration costs are all the more reason to shop at a nonwedding store for your white or cream number. Classic wedding dresses aren't the only duds that will do the trick walking down the aisle.

The Nonwedding Dress

*I*f you're set on a Cinderella confection, composed of tulle, beads, lace, and a ten-foot train, stop reading here. But if you're more of a modern bride who fancies a simple dress, like a thin sheath dress or an A-line number—or even a dress that you might have the option of wearing again—you should consider steering

Wedding Chic Word to the Wise:
Don't Size Yourself Up

It's a little-known fact in the bridal-gown biz that many women get suckered into buying a gown that's too big for them to bump up alteration prices. When the dress comes in, the bride is swimming in it . . . and then drowning in alteration fees. Don't get bullied. You know your body. Don't get talked into buying a larger size "just in case" you put on a few pounds. Chances are, with the stress of the wedding planning, you're more likely to take off a few.

clear of bridal gown salons altogether. Forgo the fancy salon and hit high-end boutiques instead. You'll get more for your money. Here are a few options beyond the pale of the average bride:

• **Buy a bridesmaid's dress.** It can come in white—or cream—or whatever you desire. It comes in the design you've been eyeing, whether that is strapless or spaghetti-strapped or tank-topped. And it costs hundreds rather than thousands of dollars. Where are the cons here? Stores like Nicole Miller have great options in classic styles for bridesmaid dresses that would fool any groom. Some shops, though, have caught on and are trying to make this savings tough to score. For example, *The Wall Street Journal* reported in June 2003 that Vera Wang's bridesmaid shop in New York City won't sell single bridesmaid's gowns in white or cream. (The CEO, Chet Hazzard, explained that translucent colors "require an extra layer of lining" and cost more to make.)

• **Buy a red carpet–worthy ensemble.** Sure, you'll be walking down the aisle instead of a red carpet, but you can still work it like Gwyneth. In fact, many numbers you see on primped-up stars would work perfectly on the nontraditional bride. As long as you're budgeting to spend a lump sum on a beautiful gown, why not devote your dollars to a truly regal dress rather than an overpriced flimsy one? Plus, then you'll actually have something to wear to one of the many black-and-white balls in your future.

Budget Bridal Gown–Shopping Strategies

• **Rent-a-Dress.** Chances are, no matter what you tell yourself, this is a piece of clothing you are destined to wear only once. So why not acknowledge that at the outset and simply borrow a dress? Shops like One Night Affair in Hollywood lend out designer gowns by folks like Vera Wang, Badgley Mischka, and Carolina Herrera for as low as $100 a night. Talk about a true Cinderella fantasy. You can return the luxurious gown at the stroke of midnight—or the next day. Glass slippers not included.

• **Be your mother's daughter.** Nothing would make her happier than seeing you swathed in her mass of puffy lace. But just because you don't like the retro design doesn't mean you have to give up on wearing your mother's vintage wedding dress. Instead, take it to a talented seamstress and see what she can do to recreate it to your liking. Almost everything can be tweaked, trimmed, and taken in. For a price.

• **Consignment.** You might immediately think consignment is old and fusty, but many brides have met with serious success diving through the racks. Head to the fancier regions of your town, where the elite unload their wares. And beware that anything you buy will require a good—and probably pricey—cleaning. So factor that into the price tag, however stunningly low. Who knows, though, you could get lucky and find just the perfect dress in exactly your size!

• **eBay.** Punch in the Web address and search out your favorite designer. This is where you'll find wedding dresses reincarnated for their second lives. And in some cases, this is where runaway brides or those who have called it off at the last minute unload their sentimental bridal baggage. Savings can really vary, but expect to get at least 25 percent off the retail price. You can also use eBay for design ideas before crafting your own dress. "I browsed on eBay for a long time," says Lynn Harris, a writer for *Glamour* magazine and the creator of

Breakupgirl.net. "It helped me know what I wanted, a nineteen-thirties bias-cut vintage gown. I bought fabric for three hundred and fifty dollars and found this awesome woman who had been working as an assistant to a couture designer. It was a little bit of a leap of faith, but I paid one hundred and fifty dollars!"

• **Sample sale.** These mongo sales are where designers unload gowns that they constructed to test out a new style, fabric, or cut. Most of these sales happen in New York City, but given potential savings of up to 80 percent off, non–New Yorkers might want to consider a trip. Check out websites, like www.nysale.com, for the best listings. Dana, a magazine editor in New York City, handled shopping for her wedding dress as if it were a commando mission. And she accomplished just what she needed to do! She showed up at 6 a.m., three hours early, to the Vera Wang sample sale in Manhattan, and ended up plucking up the perfect frock at a beautiful price. "It was like one-hundredth of retail."

• **Online.** Some websites can help you locate a budget sample gown from fabulous designers. For example, Bridepower.com and Bridesave.com are two sites that offer cut-rate sample prices on all kinds of gowns. On one site I recently found a brand-new Vera Wang A-Line dress for $1,500 that was originally priced at $2,900. Also, you can be a do-gooder while doing yourself a budgeting favor: Head to Makingmemories.org, a website for Brides Against Breast Cancer. The organization collects donated used gowns as well as new designer numbers and sells them at dozens of charity wedding-gown sales across the country for prices from $50 to $1,000. Best of all: The profits go toward breast cancer research.

• **Discount Bridal Service (DBS).** Many wedding consultants swear by this company, which promises to find the gown you're looking for and charge you 20 percent to 40 percent off the retail price. Here's how it works: You e-mail them the manufacturer's name, style number, and color of the dress you would like. They get back to you with a price quote. If the price is to your liking, they ship you the gown in the size you request. Granted, this business would require a little more faith than going to your local salon, where you can see exactly what you're buying, but isn't getting married mostly about establishing trust anyway? You should be warned that

Wedding Chic Word to the Wise:
The Fantastic Filene's Basement Sale

If you're not afraid of going head to head with ballistic brides-to-be, you might want to check out one of the nation's most famous bridal-gown sales at Filene's Basement in Boston. They have a regular bridal bonanza there. My friend Dana tried her luck and scored an amazing dress for an insanely low price. The scene is reminiscent of Spain's Running of the Bulls, except that the animals lined up outside the doors before the sale opens are women trying to score cheap wedding dresses. The foaming at the mouth is the same. Consider it the Running of the Brides. As the doors open at 8 a.m., the crowds race in and the mass becomes one big scene of elbows jarring, white dresses flying, mothers shrieking, and girls tugging. *Ole!*

returns might be a little tricky. The folks behind the company are hard to get on the phone, and their language on returns is a little vague: "Should you discover a problem," they write on their website, "simply contact the dealer who placed your order and the necessary steps will be taken to make it right for you." Which means . . . ?

• **RKBridal.** This mail-order discounter, which can be found online at www.RKbridal.com, promises to find you the gown you've set your sights on for at least 5 percent off the retail price. But beware: There are no returns and no exchanges. No nonsense.

Stretch Your Budget: Have Your Dream Dress Made

If you know exactly what you want but can't seem to find it anywhere, you might consider taking matters into your own hands and hiring an expert seamstress to recreate your favorite pattern. All you have to do is bring photos or patterns to your seamstress and talk fabrics, cuts, and detailing, and you'll be good to go. The key is to know exactly what you want, from top to bottom. You might not save a ton of money at the outset, as prices can start at $1,200 to $2,000, depending on your location and the skill of your seamstress. But you'll be guaranteed to save in other ways down the line. And let's not forget that you're getting exactly what you want, which is priceless. The advantages abound:

• **You won't need as much time.** Although buying a gown at a salon will require monthly visitations for various fittings, if you're having a gown made specifically for you, the whole process should take no more than six weeks, including all the fittings. This can be a great option for those having a shotgun affair who don't want to pay "rush charges."

• **You can forget extra charges for alterations.** Because they're making it for your body from the start, there should be no extra tacked-on prices for fittings or alterations.

• **You can play the *true* designer.** Unlike the all-too-familiar experience of finding that your dress isn't quite the same as the sample you tried on four months ago, a bride who has her dress made specifically for her gets to decide—and is sure of receiving—exactly what she wants.

• **You get to put the extra material to good use.** When the seamstress ends up with a yard or two of extra fabric, you can employ them as part of the rest of the package; for example, by making a veil, creating a crafty favor for your guests, or adding detailing to your headpiece.

All the Fixin's

Well, you've finally found the threads worthy of your wedding; they're now in the process of being altered, cleaned, and purred at occasionally, as befits such expensive threads. But wait, you're not done yet!

Some bridal stores would, in fact, like you to believe that the gussying up is only beginning. And now, they proclaim, how about everything else? Your Bridal Bra? Your super-duper special Bridal Thong? Your Bridal Corset? Your Bridal Shoes? Bridal Stockings? Your Bridal Belly Bracelet?

OK, OK, take a breath. A bridal boutique may offer a special bridal thong, but really, you need to ask yourself, what makes this strip of fabric any more "bridal" than the strip found in your local lingerie department? Is it really worth an extra $40? The answer, quite simply, is no. Here's the scoop on some of the other pieces of the bridalwear package:

Veils. I actually opted to forgo wearing a veil, much to my grandmother's chagrin. "What?" she asked me, with a pointed raise of the eyebrows. "No veil!? Come on, how about just a little something on the top of the head?" While many brides feel that the white headpiece really completes the look ("Noooww I'm a bride!"), I just didn't understand why I would need it. It felt theatrical to me. Michael and I had already been living together for two years. The virginal business would clearly be a farce. But many, many women disagree with me and enjoy the sensation of completing the bridal look with a veil.

Whatever you choose to do, this is one place where you shouldn't be spending a ton of money. You'll be wearing the veil only at the ceremony, so it's not worth spending thousands on imported fabric and diamond accents. However, it's tough to find veils at prices commensurate with what they're worth. A piece of tulle and comb should cost, at most, $50. But even at bridal superstores, you can expect to pay at least $150, and that's for the low-end veils that are sure to give you a headache by pressing into your temples. Forget it! If you're having your dress made, simply ask your seamstress to whip up a veil using leftover fabric, for about $50. Or even the most craft-impaired person can make her own. Buy a few yards of tulle for $1 to $4 a yard. Trim it with ribbon and a glue gun. Attach it to a comb, and voila! If even that scares you, buy a veil-making kit, which comes with a barrette and step-by-step instructions for making your own headpiece. You can find one on websites like www.ivillage.com.

es. There is absolutely no reason for you to buy wedding a bridal store. You'll spend an unnecessary sum for flimsy ____ and cut-rate construction, all for a cheap satiny pair. Instead, shop around at your run-of-the mill department stores or discount shoe stores like DSW. I found a pair of Vera Wang wedding shoes at a discount department store in New York City called Century 21. They needed a vigorous cleaning, which cost $20, but it was still worth it since the shoes cost $69.

Whatever you do, avoid stores that specialize in bridal shoes. At one bridal shoe store in New York City, a pair of Stuart Weitzman shoes cost $20 more than the list price on the same exact pair of shoes at Nordstrom.

Unmentionables. I can't think of one good reason why a girl would need a special Bridal Bra or Bridal Thong. If you're looking to splurge on a surprise for him later, go to a chic shop that doesn't deal in all things bridal, like La Perla or Agent Provocateur. The prices may be just as high, but you'll get infinitely better quality for your money. And the beautiful luxuries will continue to be appropriate well past the honeymoon.

Purse. Hello? Do you really need a purse? My mother was really interested in my borrowing one of her beaded purses. It remained on the table the entire night. I don't think I picked it up or carried it once, except to put it in a larger bag so my parents could take it home while I took off to an afterparty. There is simply no reason that you need to buy a special beaded bridal purse.

Jewelry. Depending on your dress and the way you plan to wear your hair, you'll want to decide between jewelry that is subtle and jewelry that attempts to make a statement. Since my dress and hair were both so clean-looking and simple, I took it as my opportunity to wear something a little daring. I had my friend Jane, a jewelry designer whose line, Linea Nervenkitt (www.nervenkitt.com), is a *Lucky* magazine favorite, custom-make a pair of earrings adapted from one of her designs. They were citrine drop earrings held together with silver. The effect was stunning. And I've been able to wear them numerous times since, because they don't scream "wedding." Don't just automatically believe you must wear pearls because it's a wedding. Take this as a fun chance to purchase a beautiful, iconic necklace or pair of earrings.

Perfume. At a wedding fair I went to a few months into our engagement, a speaker from *Martha Stewart Weddings* magazine was proclaiming the absolutely compelling properties of getting a special perfume to wear, for the first time, at your wedding. The sense of smell is so powerful, she said, that your husband will forever be pulled back into the wonderful emotions of the event when you wear it later, at anniversaries and beyond. I've always been a fan of nice perfumes, and when I graduated from college I was long overdue for settling on my Signature Scent, a fragrance that people would always associate with me. I would walk . . . it would waft. So it made sense to wear something different at my wedding. But I couldn't fathom buying a whole big perfume just for the day. Pricey! So I went to a department store, shopped around for the one that most appealed, and got a sample. Those little vials go a long way.

Commissions

One of the many reasons that you can save so much at a sample sale or online is that there are no fawning salespeople cooing over your every move, bringing you sparkling water and cookies, and high-fiving each other behind your back when you're about to take the purchase plunge. One of the reasons that the mass of tulle is priced so high is because the elevated prices incorporate high commissions for those attendants.

You may want to believe a saleswoman when she says that she's never seen someone look so fantastic in this dress, that this dress was made for you, or that you have the body of Halle Berry. Sure, you can believe her all you want. But you should also believe that she has quite a living to make from selling you this dress. Bridal-store commissions are a closely held secret in the wedding business. No one wants to talk about it. But the fact is, when you have the big "B" stamped on your forehead, salespeople can make a huge profit off you.

There are two kinds of commissions, according to Peter Grimes, the publisher of *Vows* magazine. Bridal-store salespeople can either make a straight salary or make a smaller salary with a "bump" based on performance. And that bump can be fairly big. How big?

Wedding-dress salespeople generally pull in between 2 and 5 percent commission on each sale, explains Mara Urshel, the author of *How to Buy Your Perfect Wedding Dress* and the president of Kleinfeld. If they tell you that they don't make a commission on you, she notes, they're lying.

An article in the *Los Angeles Times* on February 4, 2002, cites a wedding consultant from David's Bridal announcing just how much this can amount to. At that store, according to Debbie Schuchmann, a retailer, consultants start at a measly $8 an hour. But with an 8 percent commission, those numbers jump as high as $40 to $50 an hour during the peak months from January to August. Now just think about how much of that is coming out of your pocket. If those are the numbers at a mass, low-cost chain like David's Bridal, just imagine how well some of the Madison Avenue shop girls are doing.

Peter Grimes estimates that salespeople invest an average of 10 to 14 hours on each bride, and they're seeing multiple ladies at once. You do the math.

Your Dress:
Till Death Do You Part?

hen was the last time you spent somewhere in the vicinity of several thousand dollars on an item of clothing you wore once? How about . . . never. So why should this day be any different? Yes, it is one of the most meaningful milestones in your life. And yes, the dress sets a mood—for you, your spouse-to-be, and the fawning fans. But that doesn't mean you need to make the commitment "Till Debt Do I Part" when purchasing your wedding dress.

In fact, more and more brides these days are opting to buy high and sell a little lower when it comes to their "I Do" duds, even hawking their old, well-laundered wedding-day attire on eBay. None other than one of the country's most vocal etiquette experts, Letitia Baldrige, the former social secretary to the White House, advised cost-conscious brides in *The Wall Street Journal* in August 2003 to "sell it, if you need the money." So there.

So how much can you get? Of course, that depends on the quality of the dress. I met one bride who was hoping to get 80 percent of the original price of her never-worn Vera Wang gown. Is that reasonable to expect? Like stains, the faster you attend to it, the more success you'll see; sell

Who Knew?

If you find a gown online, head to your local salon to try on a similar model by the same designer, if you can find it. That way, you'll know what your size will be in that designer's wares.

your dress before you've even finished your stack of thank-you notes, and you can hope to get as much as 75 percent of the purchase price.

Places to Buy— and Sell— Your Gently Worn Bridal Getup

www.eBay.com
www.Craigslist.org
www.Nearlynewbridal.com

One way to think about your dress, then, is as a rental, costing the difference in purchase and sale price. Similarly, a quick search on websites like eBay can turn up brand-new dresses for serious discounts. Since you'd have to get a new gown altered anyway, you're no worse off than you would be if you bought it straight from the shop, as long as the gown is in your size range.

Wedding Chic Word to the Wise: Bridesmaids' Dresses

While the duds you'll have your wedding-party girls wear may not come out of your budget, you still want to make sure they're not going to have to take out a line of credit to pay for an ugly, overpriced taffeta number. Just like wedding dresses, bridesmaid's duds are overpriced more often than not. But you don't necessarily have to pay that much. The *Wedding Chic* way is to be creative about how you think of all the elements in your wedding, bridesmaid's dresses included. Follow these simple pointers to get great prices for your right-hand girls:

Continued

• *Do* buy in bulk so you can ask for discounts. Many shops offer small discounts if all your bridesmaids put in an order together. If the store doesn't offer it, ask for a discount.

• *Do* consider stores that don't directly cater to bridesmaids. Who really likes lime-green taffeta, anyway? Bridesmaids dresses are, for the most part, the butt of fashion jokes. Instead of taking the rote road, scout out dresses at national chain stores like J Crew (which has a new bridal line), Banana Republic, or Ann Taylor, among others. I recently saw a very cute summery dress at Old Navy for $15 that would have been beautiful at a wedding. Why not?

• *Do* check out catalogs or websites like Bluefly.com. A cool dress is a cool dress, even if it wasn't constructed specifically for a wedding. In fact, you tend to get better prices if it hasn't been. If you're wary of sizing problems, simply check the return policy and make sure everyone measures.

• *Do* allow your bridesmaids to have some say. No one wants to be bossed around or uncooperatively squeezed into a strapless dress. Make sure any design desires you have are OK with your wedding party.

Wedding Chic Word to the Wise:
Groom's Attire

Men's options for weddingware have long been a matter of choosing between two roads: rent-a-tux or buy-a-tux. But your man may want to seize this opportunity to buy a beautiful suit instead of a tux, something that he can have forever and break out at many more occasions in the future. He can consider it a sartorial investment.

A few months before our wedding, Michael's parents bought him a beautiful dark navy blue pinstripe suit at Barneys. The purchase—a man's first Barneys suit—was as much a rite of passage as the ceremony we were about to experience.

A beautiful silk pocket square and a suave silver tie dressed up the suit so much that there was no doubt this was *event* attire. And he's worn the suit several more times since—minus the tie and pocket square. Instead of just renting a polyester number for way more than you'd expect, use that money to pay for part of a beautiful suit you can keep forever.

The Contract Basics

Before signing any credit-card slip, make sure the following points are addressed in ink:

- The name and contact info of the store and yourself.

- A specific outline of fees (fittings, alteration costs, fabric, etc.).

- The deposit due date and balance due date.

- The delivery date.

- The store's refund policy.

The Bottom Line

- Manage your own expectations about finding the "perfect" dress. Is there such a thing as the "perfect" mate?

- Familiarize yourself with what drives up the price of pretty frocks, so you can choose precious detailing wisely.

- Shop at the right time and place for considerable discounts on your dream duds.

- Learn about alteration costs—and how you can trim them.

- Think outside the box, and don't automatically go for a white, poufy dress. You can save big.

- Scout out some alternative shopping spots beyond the go-to bridal boutiques.

- Be sure to get good prices on all your other accessories and unmentionables by doing research on what these items should cost—and how you can save on them.

5 · Hair and Makeup:

Beautify All You Want Without
Paying Too Pretty a Penny

rom locks to lashes, from fitness to facials, bridal beauty seemed to me to be the simple, sweet icing on the cake.

While I sweated my way through choosing my colors, second-guessed myself about the guest list (Was I leaving important people out? Would I lose friends?), and nimbly tried to appease all parties with every single decision, I thought the small matter of bridal beauty would be hassle-free.

I've written about beauty and fitness for a number of magazines over the past several years. I can rattle off beauty tips on any variety of topics, and I've accumulated a trusty Rolodex of names of stylists. Not to mention that as a self-admitted product whore, I proudly store shelves of backup moisturizer, scrubs, and nail polish like the twentysomething grandmother-in-training that I am. As I delved into the planning process, figuring out my bridal beauty plan and lining up someone to work with was one aspect I didn't have to worry about for one second.

Or so I thought.

Months into my search, however, covered in Post-its with failed leads, I was ready to toss up my hands and resort to Chapstick and a ponytail. I was simply looking for someone to do my day of hair and makeup for less than $200. I could travel to them; they could travel to me—whatever. I was willing to do what was easiest—and cheapest. Since the wedding was to be in San Francisco on Labor Day weekend, I figured I would have ample sources on which to call. I called friends who were former beauty editors for names of their best people in the Bay. But after countless calls to get quotes ($400 and up?!) and one failed trial in which I ended up with a head full of braids twisted tightly like Medusa, I finally found the best beauty pro my scant money could buy—through a message board referral on WeddingChannel.com. I felt victorious, vindicated, exhausted by the whole affair, and eager to help others avoid my tiresome quest.

Reporting back from the beauty trenches, I'm here to say that there are reasonably priced, exceptionally talented people to hire. And I'm happy to be able to offer up everything that I learned to make sure you don't have to learn the hard way.

The Price of Beauty

*T*ake a deep breath. Beauty doesn't come cheap. If you're looking for someone to arrive poolside at your suite with rollers, dryers, polishes, and creams, it doesn't even come in the triple digits. Many private hair and makeup artists think of themselves more as *artistes*, charging prices as if their latest work were to go on the auction block at Christie's. The prices can soar higher than your blood pressure every time your mom calls.

How high? In urban areas, it can be difficult to find someone to doll you up for less than $300. One stylist in Los Angeles charges $400 for hair, makeup, lashes, and consultation. Another stylist in San Francisco offers up her services for $200 to $300—an hour. *No thanks!*

You don't need to resign yourself to forgoing food for the next month to be the most beautiful bride. The fact is that beauty is like cooking: Simple dishes are the best bets; it's only when folks try to get fancy that disaster—both in the kitchen and the salon—strikes. All you need to find is someone who can do a simple hairdo, a clean look on the face, and a teensy bit of sparkle—someone who has an airy, light touch. You can find a look that will be the most beautiful and the most budget-friendly.

Bridal Hair

*F*or some reason, the prices for bridal hairstyling can soar as high as the loftiest updo, so get ready. I called dozens of hairstylists when I was on my quest to find the best person to en-

Wedding Chic Word to the Wise: Bundle Your Beauty

While you wouldn't normally ask your hairdresser to give you a massage—or your manicurist to attend to your lipo—when it comes to bridal hair and makeup, this is a good time to kill two beauty birds with one stone. If you have one person do both your hair and makeup, you can keep your costs down. You will only have to pay one person's travel cost—if they are coming to you—you need to tip only once, and, most important, you always have more negotiating power when you are bundling purchases. Ask for more services and you'll be in a better position to request a lower total price for everything.

trust my locks to for my wedding. The funniest thing I found was that people were planning to charge me a different rate than they would my mother or girls in the bridal party. I don't know about you and your family and friends, but in my world, hair is hair is hair. And we all wanted pretty much the same things: elegant chignons or simple, sleek blowouts. So why exactly would mine cost double?

It wasn't just the fact that I was getting married in potentially pricey San Francisco. Bridal parties always pay more, wherever you live in this country. Within the bridal parties, the brides cost the most. In fact, at one spot in Boston, brides are charged double what any old lady walking in requesting an updo would pay: $100 instead of $50.

Salon stylists claim that they need to charge brides double because they spend more time with a bride than any old woman and, in essence, there is lots of fawning to be done. However, I would much rather have an efficient salon session than one that is double-priced and takes twice as long. I'm not looking for therapy, girl-talk, or wedding planning rehash. I'm looking for someone to do my hair—period. And that should take the same amount of time it takes the girl next to me who is asking for the same style.

Matrimonial Makeup

ost days, you might slap on some moisturizer, pat on some lipstick, and brush on a little eyeshadow—you're not the type of girl who can't leave the house without "putting on your face." I'm mostly a Chapstick and mascara kind of girl. When I try to dress up my face for work, my lipstick generally magically disappears within an hour. I'm always incredibly impressed by coworkers and friends who appear to have a fresh coat on at all times.

So when it came to figuring out my wedding-day makeup, I was a bit stumped. "What are you thinking of for your makeup look?" my stylist asked me. "Err . . . I'll have to get back to you," I scrambled. I called my maid of honor, Sari, my right-hand lady for all things girly, and she gave me a few key words: "dewy," "shimmery," and "sweet." It turns out they were the passwords to unlock the beauty door, and my stylist knew exactly what I wanted.

Who Knew?

When deciding on what kind of makeup look you want, consider dressing up your eyes and playing down your mouth, and the makeup will remain much longer throughout the day. As you kiss your way through the crowd—not to mention planting a big one on your man—you won't have to reapply lipstick all night long.

Similar to bridal hair, you need to be extra vigilant about not getting overcharged for your bridal makeup. For example, at one salon in Annapolis, Maryland, a bride is charged $55, while her attendants will only have to pay $40. And how different can the actual end product be? A little shimmer here, a little blush there. Done!

Ways to Weasel Out of Bridal-Beauty Surcharges

*J*ust because you happen to be a bride doesn't mean you're destined to pay bridal-beauty prices. Come on. This is *Wedding Chic*, and you are far too savvy to get suckered into overpaying for something. If you take a little time and think out your strategy, a few options will certainly slash your costs.

Pretend you're just another socialite. While in your normal day-to-day existence, attending a ball that would merit a fancy hair appointment isn't necessarily a standard affair, there are some people for whom social obligations are preceded by expensive hair appointments with men named Orlando, Frederic, or Mario. When you call to schedule your bridal hair appointment, simply pretend that you have a very important to-do that evening and that you'll need serious attention to your locks.

Pretend you're a bridesmaid. Instead of announcing, "I'm the bride and I need my hair done!" which isn't all that couth to begin with, simply share the fact that you're in the wedding party. The fact is, you actually are. Whether they choose to believe that you're a bridesmaid rather than the bride is entirely up to them!

Places to Find
Oh-So-Beautiful Deals

*I*f pretending to be someone you're not makes you a little nervous, you still have options that will soften the financial blow. The most important factor in scoring savings has to do with finding a good, well-priced professional. It is possible. You need to look in the right places and hit the phones. Here are a few good leads to get you started.

Online. After many thwarted attempts to find a reasonably priced beauty professional who was willing to do me up on Labor Day weekend (one woman actually quoted me a price of $400!), I finally resorted to hitting the message boards. I found great success in a hair and makeup forum on www.weddingchannel.com. There was an extended thread where people wrote in their recommendations for good stylists. Granted, you have no idea who you can trust on a message board, but the names were a good place to start. And I got moving, Googling away, and e-mailed the most promising people.

I contacted several stylists who were recommended by my message-board buddies and finally connected with a woman named Sherrie Long, whose demeanor—and reasonable rates—endeared me to her from the beginning. Most wedding message boards have local threads that will allow brides who are getting married in your region to swap tips and recommendations. It's a wonderful resource.

Beauty schools. If the prices you're quoted literally make you blush, you might want to think about working with someone who doesn't have the equivalent of a Ph.D. in bridal beauty. Perhaps you need to find a graduate student. Call up your local beauty college and find out if they have senior students who might be interested in working with you. You may be surprised by how low their prices are. For example, both the Los Angeles Beauty College and Pacific Beauty College charge less than $10 for makeup application and just over $20 for an updo. However, don't commit before taking stock of their previous work. Remember, you're not going to be getting a haircut or anything that drastic, so there's not too much that can go wrong, especially if you come in with a firm grasp of what you like after flipping through some bridal magazines. Locate the beauty school near you by heading to www.beautyschools.com.

Your tried-and-true stylist. You head to your favorite lady every time you're in need of a cut, so why would you overlook her at such a critical time? Your longtime stylist won't dare overcharge you for your wedding. Additionally, you have the most important thing taken care of: the trust factor. You don't need to worry about

 whether or not the new girl is going to try something crazy. My friend Karmen's sister just happened to mention to her stylist that she was getting married, and the stylist offered to do her hair free as a wedding present. Loyalty pays!

Friends of friends of friends of friends. This is the time to call on your extended network and get recommendations from even your most distant, long-lost friends. Who knows? Even that pal you haven't spoken to since high school may have just the reference for you! Ask everyone you know for their best names.

Nonbridal business professionals. The person I chose to work with, Sherrie Long, had done weddings before, but they weren't her primary business. That's what I liked about her. Sherrie works mostly in television and magazines, styling stars and models. Oddly enough, that makes her rates more reasonable, because she doesn't tack on a bridal surcharge. Best of all, she really knows how to make people "photo-ready," with a face that translates well for photos without being scary-looking in person.

To find a local beauty professional in your area who may specialize in editorial work and moonlight as a bridal-beauty pro, like Sherrie, just flip through your local city magazine. Head straight to the fine print to find out who is listed as the stylist or hair and makeup artist for your favorite photo spread. Then look up that person (Google is always helpful here, but also cross-reference with other search engines, like Yahoo) and see what they have to say for themselves. If they're not available, ask them for a good recommendation.

Makeup counter. Why not just head directly to the pros who have all the tools at their fingertips: the people behind the makeup counter?

Who Knew?

We're definitely more likely to be daring when it comes to our bridal beauty. A recent survey by the Condé Nast Bridal Infobank reported that 94 percent of women tested out beauty products before their wedding. And they stuck with their new purchases: Three years later, 88 percent reported staying faithful to those products.

Many budget brides head to a counter on the morning of their wedding and get done up for free—or for a small charge. The hidden price is that you are likely to want to buy a few items, but those will come in handy over the evening whenever you want to freshen up. You may even use those colors forever. "I went to a M·A·C makeup counter to get my colors done for my wedding," recounts Alice, a magazine editor who got married several years ago. "The makeup that they chose for me—that they taught me to use—still includes all of the colors that I'm using to this day." Going to a makeup counter also means you may eliminate more day-of stress and coordination. "Don't bother hiring a professional to do your makeup," advises makeup artist Sonia Kashuk. "That's just one more person on your wedding day who could stress you out."

Kristin Van Valkenburgh runs a bridal beauty company called Eye Do and used to work behind the counter at Nordstrom in the cosmetics department. The seasoned beauty pro recommends trying out different makeup counters in the months leading up to your wedding. Get to know the salespeople, tell them what you're interested in, and settle on the best line of makeup—and an expert applicator—before making a final appointment.

Beauty Treatments

*E*very bridal magazine has handy calendars that instruct you on what you should be doing from one year to one day before the event, from your umpteenth dress-fitting to your weekly plucking. In Dan Zevin's hilarious book about the steps one takes before going down the aisle, *The Nearly-Wed Handbook*, he riffs on women's pre-event beauty obsessions. In a list titled "Bride's One-Week Countdown," Zevin includes, among other things:

Lose 97 pounds
Get hair highlighted
Get hair lowlighted
Get hair permed
Get hair straightened
Get breast-reduction surgery (left)
Get breast-enhancement surgery (right)

Now, of course Zevin is taking things to the absurd, but primping, prettying, and gussying up are all part of the joy of getting married. You have license to pamper yourself silly. When else can you feel justified in booking a massage? And when else, really, have you needed one more?

In fact, right before you get married, if your experience is much like mine, you're likely to be a stressed-out girl with untimely blemishes and shoulder knots even an expert sailor couldn't hope to undo. It's time to turn things over to the experts. But for each service you seek, there's a high road and a low road, an unnecessarily costly way and the wiser, *Wedding Chic* way.

The Cost of Beauty Treatments Across the Country

*I*t's nice to know approximately how much beauty treatments should cost before you head to a salon for a day of beauty and get caught with your bank balance down. For each of these services, the price range depends on where you live, the length of time you will be in the salon, and the specifics of your request (i.e., hot stone or deep tissue massage?). Though the sky can be the limit for some, we're capping the range at the reasonable end of the scale here. Surprisingly, however, unlike the other services, manicures and pedicures are often cheaper in big cities (from San Francisco to Miami to New York), where budget salons abound.

Facial: $60 to $100

Massage: $1 to $2 a minute

Tanning: $12 to $24 per 12- to 15-minute session in a tanning bed and about $40 for a spray-tan session

Manicure: $12 to $25

Pedicure: $20 to $60

The *Wedding Chic* Way

here are better, wiser ways to pamper yourself without overpaying. The *Wedding Chic* bride wants the same special services,
but without the unwieldy prices. Try these innovative strategies and
options:

Facial. Whatever you do, opt for a basic facial rather than a deep
tissue, excavating, hot, or hydro-anything. You're going for restorative here. The last thing you want is to have a red, sore face. If heading to a salon is truly beyond your budget, you can pamper yourself
at home. Wash your face, steam it over a boiling pot of water, exfoli-
ate, and then apply a mud mask. Finish up with another wash and a

healthy moisturizer. Voilà! You just saved
yourself $100. I do this once a month at
home and the transformation is truly dramatic. (See the following section, about
when to schedule your facial.)

Massage. With days to go, I was desperate for someone to work out the kinks
in my back. Every pesky problem started
to manifest itself around my shoulder
blades. I could have called the local Ritz
and booked a pricey session, but I chose an equally excellent option:
I got in touch with a friend of my sister Megan, who is licensed in
massage therapy. She and her partner, who worked on Michael,
charged us $60, the lower end of a sliding scale. After a healthy tip,
we were out the door, having had an expert massage in San Francisco at suburban prices. Use your resources. Find a friend—or a
friend of a friend—who has a friend who is a masseuse. Support
your pals, and you can probably even save some money. If you don't
know anyone, call a massage school and see whether they have senior students who are looking to test their new skills. Also, try your

local gym, as their rates are often less than what is charged at spas. Whatever you do, avoid a Bridal Spa Day package, which bundles a few services and tacks on a very ugly surcharge to your beauty day.

Tanning. If you're set on amping up your skin tone to have the best contrast with your bright white dress, tan at the right times to save some money. Head to a salon at off-peak hours (usually before noon), and you can get as much as a 20 percent discount. Why not try a self-tanner to get an even better discount? One of the best just so happens to be one of the least expensive: Neutrogena's self-tanners cost less than $10 a bottle.

Personally, I don't understand the whole tanning craze. Weeks before my wedding, several of my friends asked me when—when!—was I planning on tanning. How about . . . never? I'm incredibly pale to begin with, and emerging a shade of orange in my aisle walk would be jarring, to say the least. I wasn't aiming to be a different me as a bride, just the best possible me. Tanning would have been such a dramatic transformation that I didn't even consider it.

Timing Is Everything

While a facial is a wonderful treat for before the wedding, it's not exactly the kind of service you'd want to get the day before your wedding. Some facialists consider themselves pore excavators, spelunking in the depths of your facial crevices. The result can be a blotchy mess that takes a few days to resolve itself. It's not exactly a look you want to cultivate the day of your wedding. "We used to have brides calling us the day before their weddings," recalls a friend of mine who worked at an Elizabeth Arden Red Door Salon in New York City. "The day before! We would turn them away. No way would you get a facial the day before!"

So when is a good time for a facial? Figuring out your prebridal beauty regimen is a full-time job in and of itself. A few weeks before your wedding, you'll want to sit down with a calendar and plot out your war plan. Allow me to help:

T-MINUS fourteen days: Get your hair cut. Allow this much time before the wedding so it—and you—can relax. Right after I get my haircut, I always—always—have a crying jag about how it's the worst haircut I've ever had and I'm simply traumatized. Allow yourself enough time to get over that hump.

T-MINUS one week: Get your hair colored, if you're so inclined. Roots can grow out fast, so put this off as long as possible, but still leave a week before your wedding. That way the color can settle down in time.

T-MINUS one day: Get your nails done. Make sure you haven't left any heavy lifting or crafting between now and the big day, so that you don't mess up your dressed-up digits. Opt for a neutral pale pink shade. My favorite? Essie's Sugar Daddy.

T-MINUS a few hours: get a massage, if possible, on the morning of your wedding. If nothing else, it will force you to spend a little time with just yourself and have a moment to think about what you are about to do—without the pitter-pattering of everyone else around you.

Consultations: Worth Their Weight in Gold?

*L*ike any good bride-to-be, I booked a hair and makeup consultation for one Saturday afternoon when I was going to be in San Francisco, a few months before my wedding. I had chosen an unassuming salon down the street from my parents' house. The woman came recommended by the florist we were using across the street. It was all in my parents' cute, quaint neighborhood. How crazy could the prices be?

Silly question. I walked in and (wisely) asked before I plopped into the chair. The stylist casually dropped that her fee to test out a few looks for my hair and makeup: $100. *No thanks!* I simply had her do my hair (which turned into a tangly, crazy disaster), and opted out of having her test out makeup for $50. How much of a trial do you actually need for makeup? The best part about this consultation was that after she'd tested out the loser look, and after she'd charged me, she realized that—oops!—she wasn't available for my wedding date. Not that I even wanted to use her anyway. Don't get stuck in such a situation.

What I didn't realize then was that she was on the lower end of the consultation scale. Some salons charge exactly the same price for a consultation that they charge for the real event. The thinking is that any price is worth a calm state of mind. But getting overcharged for something doesn't exactly keep me calm. And the question remains: Is a consultation really necessary?

I think not. After the disaster hair episode at my consultation, I went on a mad hunt to find another person and forgo yet another consultation ($50 plus $50 plus $50 = way too much to pay to test looks). Instead of wasting money auditioning several people, simply go with a pro whom you trust. Find a worthy person to employ after working the phones and using the handy techniques above. Then let the person you hire do what he or she does best!

I had two phone conversations with Sherrie—and I e-mailed her a picture of me so that she could get a sense of what my hair looks like. Then I just closed my eyes, crossed my fingers (and toes), and hoped for the best.

If you do choose to have a consultation, think of it like an audition. There are hundreds of people out there who could possibly have the honor of doing your hair at any time. You will be paying these people a fairly substantial amount of money. Make them prove themselves to you. And if someone starts laying on the attitude, say thank you and leave. There are enough talented, gracious people out there that you need not deal with divas.

DIY Bridal Beauty

*E*very other day of the year, you do it. You stand in front of the mirror, patting down a rogue clump of hair, removing a wayward blotch of mascara, covering up unsightly red spots. So why not trust your own time-honored skills? Well, for one thing, you need a new makeup strategy, and of course you want things to be just that much more perfect on your wedding day.

That said, there's no need to call in Jessica Simpson's $4,000-a-session hair stylist and the latest honcho from Milan to turn you from everyday to Special Day. In fact, chances are you have all the tools right at your fingertips.

DIY Bridal Hair

*M*y friend Karmen, a former beauty editor for *Health* magazine, didn't panic and rush to hire someone when she was planning her bridal beauty. Instead, she took it as a great opportunity to practice her styling skills. So Karmen started by scouring all of her favorite magazines, and settled on a loose French twist. Over the course of a few weeks, she tested out all sorts of products. Which would offer the best hold? Which had the best scent? Which didn't create the crunch effect? Finally, she found the right combo

(Aveda mousse and volumizing finisher) and got to work in front of the mirror. Karmen practiced so much that she got it down to a ten-minute operation. She was prepared, and she didn't have to be all nervous about some crazy new stylist adding a huge pouf to the top of her head.

DIY Bridal Hair Looks

*Y*our first job is to head to the Web and peruse pics of bridal hair. But tread lightly—and skeptically. For some reason, when women get married, we all feel the need to have basically the same, bizarre hairdo—what I like to call the sprouting-broccoli effect. Never before in your stylish life have you had an updo, so you think, *Why not? Do it up!* Literally. But while it may be fun to do something totally different to signify that this is a special event, why not choose a hairstyle that is actually flattering? Or at least more so than sculpting hair into crusty chunks that explode in hard tendrils out of a bun. It's really not pretty. Instead, choose a look that is more elegant, like a chignon with a side part. It's hard to go wrong with such a look—and it doesn't require so much skill that you need to call in the hair paratroopers.

Another great place to peruse for hair ideas is www.wedding-hair.com, a website created by Gretchen Maurer, the author of *The Business of Bridal Beauty*. The website sells "hair kits" for $19.95 that can make your styling a cinch. Choose the look you like, purchase a kit for that particular look, and follow the step-by-step instructions. For the most complicated 'dos, Maurer has one catch-all tip: Use a soft spray for building the updo, and old-fashioned lacquer hairspray for holding. Yes, there are some skills worth retaining from the mid-80s.

DIY Bridal Makeup

*T*he day before my wedding, I wandered into Saks in San Francisco and splurged on some Bobbi Brown lipgloss, lipliner, lipstick, and waterproof mascara—a must for such a teary time. Although I had hired a stylist to do my makeup, I wanted to have my own colors so I could replenish and reapply throughout the evening. This was a perfect opportunity to splurge on makeup from my favorite line. The fact is, I'm still using the same amazing lipstick and liner to this day. Consider your wedding a handy excuse to invest in fantastic, long-lasting quality makeup.

The question remains, however: What exactly should you buy? Sonia Kashuk, one of my favorite beauty experts, who has a wonderful affordable line of makeup at Target, offers great suggestions about what any woman would pack in her beauty bag to take matters into her own hands. What you think might feel pampering may be anxiety-producing. Instead, stock up on little luxuries that you can use now and forever. Your bridal beauty bag contents should include:

Light powder (light powder leaves skin more reflective for photos)

Pressed powder (for touch-ups)

Waterproof mascara (won't get taken down by tears)

Shimmery eye shadow ("When light and flash hit shimmer, it opens up eyes and makes you look very alive," Kashuk notes. Add shimmer on top of other colors.)

Medium-tone soft-color lipstick that is long-lasting (Karmen loves Shiseido's; it "wears like iron," she explains.)

Bridal Beauty Tips

- **One word: Waterproof.** When going into battle, you need armor on your lashes. Don't kid yourself. You will most likely shed a tear, and you don't want to look like a baseball out-fielder with dark black strips under the eye. Not pretty.

- **Rethink red lips.** Unless you want to be tied to your tube all night, what starts off as a glam look looses luster fast. Go for a softer color that will be more polished—and won't throw off your whole makeup package if it fades within a few hours.

- **Allow an hour.** Don't rush yourself when doing your makeup. Set aside a nice chunk of time so you can really enjoy the preceremony ceremony of beautifying. This can be a very intimate, special moment with your mother and the bridal party.

General DIY Beauty Tips

- **Here's one time when dirtier is better.** Be sure not to wash your hair the morning of your wedding. Oilier hair is easier to style and manage than softer, freshly washed hair.

Who Knew?

While on all other days of the year you're so good about wearing mois-turizer with sunscreen, avoid the SPF on this day, especially if your wedding is inside. Sunscreen can create an odd whiteness in photos. Unless you're having a goth wed-ding, that's probably not the look you're going for.

- **Practice makes perfect.** In addition to practicing her hairdo, Karmen also didn't wing it with her wedding-day makeup. In fact, she made a habit of practicing, and then snapping photos after each trial to see which look really translated best for the paparazzi.

• **Splurge on yourself.** Here's your chance to buy some wonderful makeup. You have the best excuse, so invest in the best.

Maintain Your Makeup

Sure, you walk out of the salon feeling fancy and fabulous. And then an hour later, after absentmindedly rubbing your eyes, inadvertently tearing up, and forgetfully licking your lips, the look starts to lose its luster. Unless you're game for makeup tattooing—which isn't exactly chic in any sense of the word—keeping makeup on for a long stretch is both an art and a science.

The Science of Maintaining Makeup

• Moisturize well before you start packing on the products, and let your skin soak in the goodness. A well-hydrated face will hold makeup longer than a parched one.

• Oil-free moisturizer and eye cream tend to hold better.

• For the longest-lasting lips, start with a layer of foundation, then add liner, then color. If you're going for a matte look, brush powder through a tissue against your lips to seal the deal.

• For your eyes, start with concealer (both below and above the lids). Then press a little powder over it and blend well. Finish with your color.

The Art Part of Maintaining Makeup

• Tuck a retractable lip brush into your bra. Turn away from crowd, remove demurely as necessary. Do your business.

• Apply lipliner, then lipstick, then lipliner, then lipstick. Repeat as necessary.

• Don't overdo concealer under your prewedding, stressed eyes. It's bound to crack, crease, and approximate the Grand Canyon on your face.

• Use an eyelash curler before applying your mascara.

A Kind-Looking Kicker: Flowers

Even if your wedding isn't hippie-themed, putting some pretty blooms in your hair is an easy, affordable way to add a touch of softness and beauty. But you want to be sure to select the flowers that won't wilt within hours.

For girls who don't want to wear a veil, like my friend Emily, a garland can add a lush, stunning effect. Emily got married on the beach in Saint Martin, surrounded by family and a handful of friends.

> **Who Knew?**
>
> Add hairspray to your hair before you put in flowers, because the spray can dry out flowers and make even the hardiest blooms wilt well before cake cutting.

First, take a measurement of your head around the crown. Gather the best flowers, including greenhouse spray roses, which are both inexpensive and long-lasting, and attach the flowers to barrettes and bobby pins. Fasten into the hair on top of your head.

Hair-Friendly Flowers

ot every type of flower does well when plucked and planted atop your head for several hours. You have to choose the choicest blooms. These flora will stay spritely on top of your sunny face—all day and night:

Stephanotis (a small white blossom so waxy that it will hold up well without water)

Spray roses and rosebuds

Tuberose blossoms

Calla lilies

Berries

Rosehips

Fresh gardenia (spritzed lightly with a tiny bit of little lemon juice to prevent browning)

Dendrobium and cymbidium orchids

Who Knew?

To ensure the longest life for your flowers, dip them in Crowning Glory solution, a milky, white liquid that coats the flowers in a transparent film that preserves them. You can find gallons of the solution at most floral-supply shops.

Forget These Flowers

lace these blooms in your locks and the clock will start ticking to wilt-down:

Open dahlias (you have only thirty minutes)

Hydrangeas (prone to shrivel)

Large lilies (can you say limp?)

Fast-Track Bridal Fitness

*Y*ou may have labored over all other parts of your looks, but fitness is the final portion of the beauty package. And many girls feel a compulsion to have instantly slimmed-down hips, a tightened midsection, and toned upper arms. (Who wants to jiggle-jiggle during the send-off wave?)

Nerves may take care of some last-minute weight loss. For example, without trying, really, I lost five pounds in the few months before my wedding. Rather than leaving your physique up to the workings of stress, why not take matters into your own hands?

Whatever you do, don't bother forking over hundreds of dollars for prewedding personal training—or even a pricey gym membership. Get your body into bridal shape by doing some free exercises at home. No over-priced equipment, no gear, no "ten easy installments of $1,495!"

One great book that can help guide you through the process is Sue Fleming's *Buff Brides: The Complete Guide to Getting in Shape and Looking Great for Your Wedding Day*. In the book, Fleming, a PE teacher at a Riverdale Country School in New York, offers virtual training through the pages. "There's no greater motivator than a wedding day," she says. But instead of racing to tone your back and upper arms to look like a knockout in your strapless dress, consider your wedding the first step toward a healthy lifestyle and sustainable workout routine.

Your Prewedding Workout Gear

• Two free weights (five or eight pounds each). Under $10 at Kmart or Target.

* A fitness ball. Less than $20 at Target.

* An alarm clock (without a snooze button) to get yourself out of bed in the morning!

Most brides-to-be are interested in focusing on their upper body, deltoids, shoulders, biceps, and triceps, notes Fleming. She advises that it is ideal to get started six months ahead of time with twice-weekly workouts. Short-term shaping up is also possible. With three months, you can achieve your goals, as long as you step up your frequency to four times a week. Whether you follow the quickie routine or the longer one, Fleming suggests that you supplement your weight work with aerobic activities, starting with 60 to 80 minutes per week at the beginning, and eventually ratcheting it up to 120 minutes per week. Here's a small sampling of what Fleming recommends in *Buff Brides*:

One Beautiful Back
(Exercises Adapted from *Buff Brides*)

When you're at the altar, all eyes will be on you—and your back! Here's how to wow 'em.

1) **Back extensions using an exercise ball.** Rest your torso/midsection on the ball with the tops of your toes on the ground. Interlock your fingers behind your head and, to the count of four, lift your chest up a few inches. Repeat 8 to 12 times per set.

2) **Swimming simulation.** Lie facedown with your arms overhead and your toes pointed. Keep your chin off the ground. Slowly raise your left arm and right leg simultane-

ously until they are both a few inches off the ground. Switch to the other side. Repeat 12 to 15 times for one set.

Sleek Shoulders

During your first dance, the spotlight, literally, will be on your shoulders as you hug your honey close to the strains of your favorite romantic/cheesy/sentimental tune. Here are two exercises to get them in shape.

1) Using two dumbbells, keep your forearms perpendicular to the ceiling. To the count of four, raise both dumbbells out to the sides and then up to head height, then lower. Try 8 to 12 reps for one set.

Wedding Chic Word to the Wise:
Don't Do InstaDiets

The worst thing you can do for weight loss is panic and go on one or all of the following: 1) the coffee diet, 2) the water diet, 3) the "I'm so busy, I just can't find time to eat" diet, or 4) the "all gummy bears, all the time" diet. You'll actually work against any gains you are making in building muscle tone, which helps your body burn more calories when it's at rest. Not to mention ramping up your stress levels and decreasing your over-all energy, which is an all-around bad idea!

2) Hold the dumbbells level with your upper abs with your palms facing your body in front of you. To the count of four, raise one dumbbell to your shoulder height. Pause, and then lower it to the count of four. Repeat with your other arm. Try 8 to 12 reps for one set.

Tricked-Out Triceps

Lying on your back on the exercise ball with your shoulders, neck, and upper back supported, keep your knees bent and your feet flat on the floor. Squeeze your butt muscles. With a dumbbell in each hand, extend your arms straight up, with your palms facing in. To the count of four, lower the dumbbells to your ears, bending at the elbows (not the shoulders). Return to the starting position. Repeat 10 to 15 times.

The Contract Basics

Before signing, make sure the following points are addressed in your contract with any beauty vendor:

• The date and time of the event.

• The name and contact info for the specific vendor who will be working with you, as well as the address where you will be meeting.

• The number of hours you have booked, and the number of people the professional will be working on during that time.

• A specific outline of all fees (including breakdown of costs).

- The deposit due date and balance due date.

- The stylist's cancellation and refund policy.

The Bottom Line

- Figure out what you're willing to spend on bridal beauty.

- Bundle your day-of beauty and hire one person for the best prices.

- Be mindful of beauty tricks to make sure your makeup looks the best and lasts the longest.

- Search out alternative vendors for the best prices.

- Prioritize your prewedding beauty treatments—and learn what each should cost.

- Don't be afraid to do it all yourself.

- Consider forgoing an expensive consultation (or two!).

- Find flowers that won't wilt for your hair.

- Learn some new moves to get in shape now—and forever.

Part 2

THE PRESENT:
THE DAY-OF DETAILS

"You shouldn't put stock in what people have to say or think. You want to throw the wedding or party that makes you happy and feeds your soul. Hopefully, the people that you invite to your wedding would be there because they want to see you get married, not because they want a thirty-five-dollar veal chop."

JEAN CHATZKY
Today Show CORRESPONDENT • AUTHOR OF *Pay It Down Today: From Debt to Wealth on $10 a Day* • AND COLUMNIST FOR *Money* MAGAZINE

6 · The Tunes:

Score Entertainers with Prices That Are Music to Your Ears

y husband, Michael, is a music writer who works at *Entertainment Weekly*, so when it came time to delegate wedding projects, having him select our wedding tunes was the obvious choice. He might not know flowers, but he can name a song and artist from the first few bars of any CD I pluck out of his well-stocked racks. Most important, he is extremely mindful about what music to play when, and what effect it has. Making dinner? Sonny Rollins. Getting ready to go out? Manu Chao. Sunday-morning newspaper reading? Erik Satie. I completely trusted him to handle the soundtrack of our reception.

At the beginning, we confronted a conundrum that all engaged couples encounter: Would we go with a band or a DJ? That small decision has large implications, as what you choose truly sets the mood. A DJ can play exactly what you want when you want it, but there's no focal point other than a guy behind some tables in a cheap tux. A band is riskier, in that they might cover your favorite tune with a large amount of artistic license, and they disappear for regular breaks, but when they're on they can enliven a room. Whatever you select, choosing the tunes for your wedding requires being extra mindful about your music. The key is to find a performer with the perfect mix: four bars of talent, two bars of attitude, and a healthy dose of confidence.

From the beginning, we had decided to go with a band rather than a DJ. A good band can set the mood in such a clear, elegant way, we concluded. But who could we find who would be good— and in our price range—from 3,000 miles away? Within weeks, under Michael's direction, we had gathered a bunch of recommended names as our leads, called in CDs and cassettes, and started swimming in glossy headshots of bands with names like the Blue Notes and Chain of Fools. Pulling out the hilarious headshots for whomever stopped by our apartment was our favorite party trick for months! "Look at her hair. . . ." Ultimately, we sent our scouts to go hear the final contender perform in a number of venues, including another wedding; we called and interrogated her references, and we said, "Hit me with your best shot."

The Big Decision: Band vs. DJ

The first thing you will have to decide when it comes to selecting the soundtrack to your union is whether you want to hire a band or a DJ. Like East Coast vs. West Coast hip-hop, the Yankees vs. the Red Sox, or salty vs. sweet, most of us have firm, divisive ideas about which rules. DJs can generally be cheaper, if only because there are fewer people to hire than there are in a several-piece band.

But remember: The *Wedding Chic* bride is most interested in getting the most band for her buck, not just spending the fewest bucks—although that can be a nice bonus. So before making a decision based solely on price, you'll want to bone up on the basics of what gives in the band-vs.-DJ debate. Each camp has its pros and cons. As with anything, you'll have to weigh your priorities and make an informed choice based on all the information you can gather. Here's a start:

Bands

PROS

- Bands can introduce boisterous, festive energy to your crowd.

- Bands can be much more memorable than DJs.

- Your resident family musicians can join along—or not!

- A band's breaks allow for easy toasting time or the opportunity to talk.

- Bands forge an emotional connection with the crowd.

CONS

- Grandma is very (very) concerned about the noise level!

- Bands can only play what is in their repertoire. Want a little Jay-Z at the end of the night? You'll have to sate that craving at the afterparty.

- The resident family musicians may feel inclined to bum-rush the stage.

- A wedding band can usually only play one—or maybe two—styles of music well. It had better be a style you like.

DJs

PROS

- A DJ can keep the music going all night long. No fifteen-minute breaks every hour, like most bands require.

- You can hear what you want to hear. Period.

- Volume levels aren't a problem. Turning it down is as simple as a twist of the knob.

CONS

- The music isn't personalized.

- There's always the threat of a DJ getting a leet-le too cozy with the mic. "Are you all ready for a little limbo???!!? Are we ready for 'We Are Family'?!?!"

• There isn't necessarily a distinction between the quality of
the music at this event and that at your last house party. DJs
can be short on that special something.

Now that you've parsed out some of the pros and cons and taken
your corner, whether it is band or DJ, you'll still need to score the
best. Here's how to narrow down the field of fools to find the truly
fabulous and home in on the hacks and the heroes.

Deciding on a Band

efore booking a band, you need to do your due diligence,
perk up your ears, listen closely to their mix, and ask the
right questions. Here are factors you should pay attention to:

• Are they in tune? Crooning with a large dose of enthusiasm
is all well and good, but a wannabe Mariah truly falls flat if
she can't hit her notes.

• Are they reliable? Get references
from previous gigs. Call those references. Ask every single question you
want, including: What did they wear?
Did they show up on time?

• Are the folks you hire going to be
the same ones who show up to perform?
One bandleader in Salt Lake City actually bragged about how
he's able to capitalize on his name and send out another band
in his place when he double-books: "There are four of me
every night!" he shared. "I'm not always there; they're clone
bands. With me, the entire band could quit and I'd still be in

business. I do volume." *Great!* Be sure to get in writing the names of the folks who will be performing so you don't fall prey to being just one of many customers who don't get what they thought they paid for.

• Are they adding unnecessary fees and members? All you need are actual players. Beware of the band that insists you need an MC in addition to the musicians. Beyond disrupting any elegant vibe you hope for, an MC tacks on unnecessary charges. Also, don't get scammed into paying tax on your band. Some brides have unwittingly paid tax or a "10 percent administrative union service charge." What's that? For one thing, it's unnecessary. Don't be fooled; there is no such thing as a tax on entertainment services, or an "administrative union charge," advises Stan Wiest, a veteran bandleader in the New York City area.

Who Knew?

Just because you're getting married doesn't mean you need to hire a "wedding" band. Hit your favorite clubs and dive bars with your ears perked for up-and-coming or over-the-hill talent. Find your favorite group and then see what they'd charge to do your event. Struggling musicians can mean super savings.

• Find out if they offer "continuous flow." The best bands will work it so the music never stops, even during breaks. They'll phase one musician in and another out, changing the mix to allow one another to rest. Meanwhile, the band plays on.

Bad-Idea Bands

Sure, you can quickly toss off who your favorite stadium bands are (the Rolling Stones, Bruce, etc.), but when it comes to wedding bands, all bets are off. Certainly, there are some clues that should tip you off about which bands to avoid. Warning signs include:

- Anyone with themed costumes

- Big, teased hair

- Chattiness between sets

- Sexpot sixty-year-old front-women or -men. *Ay.*

Scoring the Richest Sound, Piece-by-Piece

Of course, flying in a twelve-piece funk band from Detroit would be an ideal arrangement. But for those of us with an eye on the bottom line, that's probably not financially feasible. So how do you determine how many pieces you want to hire for your band? The key is to find the best combinations and to get the richest sounds with the fewest musicians. First of all, the number of pieces in your wedding band should relate to the number of guests you expect to attend the reception. Basic rule of thumb: The more guests, the bigger the sound you'll need, because bodies absorb noise. The following general guidelines apply:

For less than 85 guests: a three-piece band
For between 85 and 100 guests: a four-piece band
For 100 or more guests: a five- to six-piece piece band
For more than 175 guests: a six- to eight-piece band, and up

The Best Arrangements for the Smallest Price

*I*n addition to choosing a space that will be budget-friendly for your music choice, you can also save some precious money by hiring the right *kind* of musicians and maximizing your budget by getting a boost in sound. For example, paying for two singers wouldn't be exactly the best way to allocate funds if you only want to hire a four-piece band. You'd be heavy on vocals and light on important instrumentals.

Affordable Arrangements

For a one-piece band: trumpet player or singing pianist (Note: good for a small room)
For a two-piece band: a singing keyboardist and drummer
For a three-piece band: a singing keyboardist, drummer, and bass player
For a four-piece band: a singer, keyboardist, drummer, and bass player
For a five-piece band: a singer, keyboardist, drummer, bass player, and guitarist
For a six-piece band: a singer, keyboardist, drummer, bass player, guitarist, and saxophonist
For a seven-piece band: a singer, keyboardist, drummer, bass player, guitarist, saxophonist, and trumpet player
And up: add an extra singer . . .

The Cost of Adding a Band Member

ow much does it cost to add members? Bands generally charge about $100 to $300 an hour extra to add a member. For example, while the infamous bandleader in Salt Lake City who double-dips might charge $2,775 for a six-piece band for three hours, a ten-piece band would set you back in the neighborhood of $4,225.

Wedding Chic Word to the Wise: Music-Friendly Venues

Believe it or not, the venue you choose can actually affect how much money you'll need to spend on your band. How? Depending on the décor and the makeup of a room, the space will have a direct bearing on how sound carries. Having the wedding outside, on the beach, or in Mom and Dad's backyard will require not only tents but also a few extra musicians to provide a big enough sound. Meanwhile, the ballroom at the local hotel downtown can be kinder on your band budget, thanks to a wood dance floor and walls that deflect sound. Also, beware that the bigger your wedding, the bigger the band you'll need, because all those third cousins absorb that much more sound. One more reason to limit the guest list from the beginning!

Deciding on a DJ

The last time you hired a DJ was . . . never. So how do you find the best? Wedding DJs are a notorious bunch of cheeseballs. When sifting through the mix, pay attention to these factors to find your diamond in the rough:

• Do they let you dictate the set list? For the musically attuned among us, part of the appeal of hiring a DJ is having absolute control and knowing you'll get to hear exactly what you want. So why not take it to the umpteenth degree and actually tell them the order of things, from "It Had to Be You" at the start to Sade at the end? If this is your inclination, make sure you hire someone who doesn't have his own (firm) ideas about things.

Who Knew?

How much can you actually save by turning your music over to a DJ instead of a band? Try 40 percent. It's not an insignificant sum!

• Would they do your cocktail hour as well? Some DJs are willing to work out a package deal, including four hours at the reception and background music during the cocktail hour. You can save hundreds of dollars by negotiating to have your DJ handle the whole affair.

• Ixnay on the skits, dance instructions, interactive games, or lighting packages. There's no room for the chicken dance at a chic wedding. Period.

• Can they keep things simple? You're hiring someone to handle the music, not play comedian or entertainment whiz.

Politely dismiss anyone who fancies himself a pseudo-Seinfeld and plans to literally claim center stage during your wedding.

Don't Do It DJs

*C*hances are, you're not going to be able to afford Mix Master Mike of the Beastie Boys or Moby. But taking things a few notches down carries a little risk. Things can get ugly with wedding DJs—fast! Beware of these EZ Cheeze Markers of DJs:

- Smoke machines

- Mullets

- Plastered-on fake smiles

- Bubbles

- Glitter

- Dancers to work the crowd

- Flashing lights

- Scratching (*wicky, wicky . . .* whoa . . .)

Multitasking Musicians: The DJing Bandleader

*Y*ou may be surprised to know that you don't have to choose between a band and a DJ. Michael and I hired a bandleader named Joni Max, who offered to spin while the band took its breaks. That way, the music would be continuous. Before the wedding, Michael made a CD with all of our favorite hits—the songs we really wanted to hear at our wedding but didn't want a wedding band to attempt (including songs by Prince, Parliament, the Pharcyde, and so on). Sure enough, when the band took its breaks, the adults would as well, hitting the deck for a time-out drink. The young folks among us hit the floor to bust a move to R. Kelly, Sean Paul, and the Fugees. At the end of the night, everyone had heard the music they wanted to hear. If you truly can't decide, try to find a bandleader who can play both roles. All it requires is the ability to press PLAY on a CD player.

Book 'em! Why Timing Is Everything

*L*ike all other aspects of your big shebang, timing is key to get the most for your money. And hiring musicians is no different.

• **Avoid the holiday season.** Musicians can easily get booked up during the holiday season, so they can justify charging higher rates. Although a band generally makes its bread and butter at weddings, you might find that the folks you're interested in hiring for your December event are already fully booked. If they are available, because they can count on being hired at other parties, they may also hike their prices.

• **Do research about what's happening where you are choosing to have your wedding.** If you're getting married in a town that cashes in on drawing conventioneers, make absolutely sure that you're not going to be competing for space and entertainment with the National Association for Hefty Casket Sales. Just head to the website of the major convention center and check dates. Competition hikes prices—for bands as well as for venues.

Wedding Chic Word to the Wise: Take Recommendations from the Venue

Here's one time when it can really behoove you to take advice—or names—from the venue coordinator. Bands that have played at your venue will know exactly how the room affects the sound, setup will be a snap, and therefore you can be sure the first several songs won't be trial-and-error—on your dime. Be sure to check with your venue coordinator to get names of recommended musicians, and then start your selection from that group of band options.

- **Think off-season.** January may not be your ideal time to get married, but when you see how much you can save for the same services, you might warm up to the idea of a winter wedding. Stu Hirsh, a bandleader in Chicago, says he charges $1,500 less for a January wedding than a June wedding, slashing prices from $6,500 to $5,000 for a ten-piece band for three hours on a Saturday night. That was certainly appealing for Karen, who planned a January wedding in New Hampshire. She saved $600 on her DJ.

The Chic-est Ceremony Music

Who Knew?

Although Michael and I thought we were being savvy by booking a band months in advance, we learned that by doing that we lost some negotiating power. Since our band wasn't desperate for the gig, they didn't bite when we asked if their rate was negotiable. And why should they? Four months out, chances are they probably would have gotten another offer at their standard rate. Here's one situation when having less time can pay off. If a band has an opening for your date a month out, don't accept the first price they list. You're actually in the power seat when you book a band at the last minute. After all . . . what's their other option? Jamming in their living room for free?

Remember, this whole wedding business isn't all fun and games. Before you get to work up a sweat on the dance floor, you have to earn that right at the altar. And your music during that equally important time should be just as beautiful. You'll want to have equally affordable—and elegant—music to provide just the right vibe as you walk down the aisle. To keep your costs down, choose a sound that's rich in tone but affordable in price. Why not consider these options (from lowest cost to most expensive)?

Acoustic guitar

Piano (make sure to confirm that a piano will be available)

Church organ

Solo clarinet

Piano/flute

Piano/flute/trumpet

Wind trio

String trio

String quartet

Who Knew?

If you are getting married in a church, why not go local with your music: Use an organ. Churches will often have an organist they use. Be sure to ask how much they charge before signing up. Perhaps you can ask for it to be included as a "value added." It's worth a shot!

Hidden Cost: Harps

f nothing says "wedding" to you like an ethereal harp, then steel yourself for a price hike; harpists can charge as much as 25 percent more than their pianist pals. In fact, standard fees range

Wedding Chic Word to the Wise: Due Diligence Before You Book

This is one time when it's actually kosher to crash someone else's wedding. When you're deciding on a band, find out if they have any upcoming gigs. Oftentimes, you can be invited to stop by and check out their tunes and moves. Just don't partake in any of the hors d'oeuvres.

from $250 to $450 to accompany your jaunt from Dad's elbow to your husband's lips, a thirty-minute affair. One reason: Harps are so large, just transporting them requires that they be trucked in. Though harp music may wrench out a few more tears and gasps from your friends and family, it's probably not worth your while. Add your elegance in different areas.

Measures to Save Money on Your Music

• **Time wisely.** As with your venue, and hundreds of other components in this event, timing is everything in getting a good deal on great services. Here is yet another place you can save by having a wedding at any other time than on a Saturday night. For example, on Saturday or Sunday afternoon weddings, you can factor in saving as much as $100 per musician, according to Ian Magid, the event producer at Hank Lane Music and Productions, one of New York's most popular wedding-band coordinators. (They represent ten bands and two orchestras, coordinating 50 to 100 weddings a month!)

> **Who Knew?**
>
> Don't bother going for a string quartet when a string trio can do practically the same job. An excellent trio, including a violin, viola, and cello, will be able to handle the same repertoire as if they had the extra violin. And the reduction in sound from four to three is disproportionate to how much more you'd have to pay for the extra musician.

• **Go small-scale.** Even if you decide against a DJ, that doesn't mean you need to plan on hiring a twenty-five-person orchestra. Try to get the richest sound for your dollar. But also consider a skilled one-man band. Technology can take over where manpower ends. With sequencing, drum machines, and keyboard bass, one man can sound like five.

This works especially well at weddings with fewer than fifty guests, and those where dancing isn't necessarily in the plans. That's because one man doesn't necessarily incite the same drive to dance as a full stage of players.

• **Hire multitasking musicians.** Instead of hiring separate folks to play at your ceremony, cocktail hour, and reception,

---

Wedding Chic Word to the Wise:
Cost-Saving with Your Cocktail Hour

Don't waste your precious funds by hiring separate musicians for the cocktail hour. Amid all the kiss-kissing, crying, and sloshing of drinks, no one is even going to notice, much less pay attention to, that quiet vocalist working it in the corner. However, if you insist on having a tinkling musical background, at least go for something that will carry over the rising roar, like a live piano rather than two acoustic guitars or a wind trio.

The string trio that played our ceremony continued to play during the cocktail hour (mostly because we had them for a certain amount of time, and why not squeeze the most out of 'em?). But once the drinks started clinking, no one could even tell that there were musicians in the room. Be assured that if your pennies are running short, musical accompaniment during cocktail hour is an easy, seamless place to cut costs without anyone noticing or the whole wedding being considered a big bust!

consider the pre-party action just a subset of your big band that plans to debut at dinner. For example, hire one pianist or flute-playing saxophonist (many saxophone players are proficient on the flute) to play at your ceremony. Another option is to have your band's guitarist go unplugged—and classical. You'll only need to pay them a couple hundred extra rather than hiring completely separate musicians, the prices for whom can start at $400 and rise quickly.

• **Save with students (or teachers).** We found the musicians to play at our ceremony by calling the San Francisco Community Music Center, where I had taken voice lessons when I was in high school. We hired a trio of stringed-instrument instructors for a great price. Most local music schools, from community centers to conservatories, are eager to hook up students and teachers with those looking for some performers. Some spots, like the New England Conservatory in Boston, have a line you can call to make the connection. Look in your local phone book for the music school near you.

DIY Music

Sure, you could hire the Rolling Stones to play your wedding. But realistically, you're working on a much lower scale. When you pare down and really start crunching numbers, you might want to consider the lowest cost, highest-yield option of all: hiring your musically inclined friends and family to play at your wedding.

My friend Lisa is a semiprofessional clarinet player and comes from a family of musicians. So there was no question at her wedding: her little sister Amy, also a bridesmaid, would play while Lisa walked down the aisle. It required a little extra stage presence for Amy not to choke up while watching her big sis appear in full bridal regalia, but she held it together with panache and played a beautiful refrain. Lisa saved a few hundred dollars by enlisting the help—and talent—of her sister. In a similar scenario, you'll be surprised how honored some people might be to be asked to take on such a meaningful role at your wedding.

That's all well and good for the ceremony, but how about the reception? Well, if you just so happen to have friends in a brilliant klezmer band, you're certainly in luck. But for those of us not as stunningly hooked up, there is still a wonderful option: DIY DJing.

Enlist a B-list friend—one whom you wouldn't really want to be spending all that much quality time with at your wedding, anyway—to coordinate the tunes at your wedding reception. Contrary to popular belief—or viewings of the movie *Scratch*—your friend doesn't actually need to have mad skillz on the ones and twos to call himself a DJ. In fact, make things easy by setting him up with a strict set list and some rented equipment costing no more than $200 a night. Your friend will be ready to go. Don't worry about rounding up turntables; for the purposes of your wedding, a well-stocked MP3 player or a pair of CD players and a mixer will actually be ideal for the sake of ease. Just be sure your DJ pal is well taken care of by the bartenders and buy him a nice gift in thanks.

What you'll need to rent:

• A small PA (public address) system, which should include two self-powered speakers on stands, an amplifier, and all necessary cabling

- One wireless mic

- Electrical cabling

- An eight-foot table for a laptop, CD player, or two turntables for records

If you'd like to simplify things even further, just borrow a friend's well-stocked MP3 player and connect it directly into an amplifier. Plug it all in and play away. Beware: You'll want whoever will be manning the music to test all the equipment and the sound system well before the event to familiarize himself with how the program works. Be sure to check with your venue about any possible restrictions before investing in equipment.

Are Agents a Good Idea?

*H*iring your band through an agent might seem deceptively easier at the outset: *I'll just call this one guy and get him to send me a bunch of CDs of potential bands!* But the fact of the matter is that an agent can seriously complicate things for you—and hike prices. In fact, agents generally add at least 20 percent to your total music budget. You'll have to decide how much the convenience is worth.

If you do decide to pay more to be led to a stable of available bands, be warned that wedding-band agents have a number of groups that they're trying to sell at any one time. When you call requesting a five-piece rock-and-roll band (*they have to know "Brick House!"*), the agent may end up trying to sell you on his seven-piece funk band, just because that's the band that's available on your wedding date. While his goal is hiring out whomever he's got, it's not necessarily in line with your goal: hiring the best possible band for you.

Whatever you do, know that these guys negotiate, and you should never take the first price they offer. If they're pretending that they won't budge, ask for extra services, like an extra hour tacked on for free or for one of the musicians to play during your ceremony.

Agent Do's and Don'ts

• **Hire like with like.** Don't fall into the trap of one-stop shopping with your wedding music. While one agent may offer to hook you up with your ceremony and reception music, chances are that you'll want two very distinctive styles. Clas-

Wedding Chic Word to the Wise:
Overtime Hours

The party's rolling, and you don't want it to end. How much will it cost you to extend the festivities? Many bands charge a bundle for extra time, and it ranges from 75 percent of their normal hourly rate to an hourly fee of $50 to $100 per band member. For a small four-piece band, that extra hour can come to an extra $400.

Most bands you hire will be playing for four hours, and that should be plenty. The party-pleasure return on that fifth hour will be disproportionate to the extra amount you will have to pay. End your party on a high note so that you'll simply stow away mental snapshots of what fun you had rather than dragging things out to the truly exhausted end.

sical musicians aren't going to be as good when they come with an agent who specializes in klezmer.

• **Make sure you're getting who you paid for.** Just because you hire a band based on the musicians who played on the CD you heard doesn't mean you'll necessarily get those same players on your wedding day. Be sure to specify in your contract the names of the musicians who will be playing at your wedding. The advantage to using an established band instead of newcomers is that the established band's set is often much tighter and well rehearsed. You will definitely notice the difference.

• **Be certain you're insured in case of emergency.** If, God forbid, something happens to your band before your wedding, going through an agent can be beneficial to you. They'll find you a substitute at the last minute. It may not be your first choice, but it'll be better than the next best option: karaoke.

• **Remember, an agent is a salesperson.** You want funk? They've got an "amazing funk band perfect for you!" You want rock? They've got "the best rock band in the greater Denver area!" Remember to be a little skeptical, listen, and ask lots of questions.

Michael's "Do Not Play" List

After you hire someone and pass on some of the control, it's critical to give your musicians guidance about what you like—and, more important, what you don't like. Michael and I met with our bandleader for coffee before the wedding. Michael came prepared with three lists: Definitely Play, Do Not Play, and If You

Dare Play This I Will Personally Come Drag You Off the Stage. Of course everyone considers himself a musical expert—and everyone has different taste. But all of the following songs made our Do Not Play list. Feel free to follow our lead:

"Brick House"
"Love Shack"
"Greatest Love of All"
"That's What Friends Are For"
"Hot, Hot, Hot" by Buster Poindexter
"Jump, Jive, and Wail" by Brian Setzer
Any Elton John, Celine Dion, Mariah Carey, Whitney Houston, or Barbara Streisand songs
Any Village People songs

The Contract Basics

efore signing, make sure the following points are addressed in your contract:

* The date and time of the event.

* The names of and contact info for specific musicians who will be performing.

* The hours they will be hired for.

* The hourly rate for overtime charges.

* The specifics of setup and breakdown.

* A specific outline of fees (including a breakdown of costs).

• The deposit due date and balance due date.

• The cancellation and refund policy.

The Bottom Line

• Start by deciding between a DJ and a band by parsing out the pros, cons, and average prices for each.

• Follow guidelines to figure out the smallest number of band members you will need to get the richest sound. More musicians equal more money.

• Set guidelines for what you will and will not allow your DJ to do and play.

• Try to find the best of both worlds: a DJing band leader. They exist.

• Consider cost-effective options for your ceremony music.

• Learn creative measures to save money on your music.

• Don't be afraid to hire talented friends or neighbors.

7 · The Flowers:

Get the Most Bloom for Your Buck

here's truly nothing like fresh flowers to enliven a room. When it comes to weddings, a room bursting at the seams with fragrant blooms instantly infuses luxury into the event. As with any choice in your wedding, you can maximize your bloom budget in easy ways, achieving elegance without over-spending.

It would be easy simply to opt for roses. Roses, roses, roses, as far as the eye can see. But roses are the rote, easy road in wedding flowers. In fact, roses are to weddings what Kleenex is to tissues, Xerox is to copies, and Starbucks is to coffee: the big name but not necessarily the best choice all the time. With the big name often comes the *venti grande* prices as well.

On my first visit to meet the florist I'd hired to do my wedding, I found my head spinning with new terms. His first question threw me for a loop: "OK, so what are your colors?" *My colors? Err . . .* I'd never been asked my colors before. "Well, I'm pretty pale, and I have blue eyes," I wanted to say.

From there, things went downhill quickly. Sensing how green I was with the whole wedding-flora biz, he started spitting out tons of lingo: "Well, you could do calla lilies and gerbera daisies mixed with lemon leaves here, with a hint of hydrangea—or we could pack the room with dahlias. Yes, yes, that might be nice. Or actually some sweet peas and peonies. Sound good?"

"Errr . . . sounds good to me!" But like an aggressive sommelier, it is a trick of the trade to show who is boss. Not everyone is as intimately familiar with the visual difference between spray roses and regular roses, between dahlias and dendrobium orchids. And unless you work at *House & Garden* or the local nursery, you shouldn't be expected to.

Now that you're in the market for the best flowers for your wedding, it's your job to become an insta-expert. Don't wilt under a barrage of lingo and acquiesce to whatever your florist flings your way. Instead, come armed with your own options. If you don't know your colors (in other words, if you don't have a general sense of the palette you plan to use for your dress, table linens, cake, and so on), you still can be equally prepared with the necessary knowledge. And with a little flora expertise under your belt, you'll be set to squeeze every drop out of whatever funds you have to spend on your flowers and plants.

Choosing the Most Fabulous Florist

Selecting the right person to hire to provide the floral touches for your wedding is a big decision. Settle on the guy who works right next to the supermarket, and you might just find yourself awash in drooping blooms mere minutes into the big day. This doesn't mean you should head to the most famous florist who handles all the black-tie events in town. There is a wonderful and inspired middle ground. Your job is to find it. Beyond being well stocked with blooms, the best florist will:

- **Be able to explain the different options.** Don't be shy about asking what a calla lily looks like. Not everyone spends their working lives with their noses pressed up to big blooms.

- **Be flexible on price.** Just because he or she might not drop their price when you ask doesn't mean your florist can't be flexible in other ways. For example, instead of letting them take the reins right at the beginning, start your negotiations on the right foot. When my mother and I walked down the street from my parents' house into the shop of the florist who ultimately did our wedding, my mother's first words were, "You couldn't do my daughter's wedding for under two thousand dollars, could you?" Their answer? "Of course we can!" Instead of immediately being led to elaborate, pricey options and arrangements, we started from the other direction and worked backward, only brainstorming about what was feasible and reasonable.

• **Be quick on his or her toes.** The best florist will help you maximize your budget by offering to do what is called a "market buy." You will settle on a wide range of options of types of flowers that could work ahead of time. The florist will also know your color scheme. Then, the day of the big event, the florist will go buy whatever is on sale at the market, within your guidelines. That way, he can pass the savings on to you!

Supermarket, Not Downmarket

You may trust them for your frozen peas and carrots, but when it comes to your wedding flowers, hitting your local Stop 'n' Shop might not be the first thing that comes to mind. Surprisingly enough, it's worth seriously considering. At your local supermarket, you can expect to see the same quality flowers you see at your local fancy florist—for far lower prices. Because supermarkets buy flowers in larger volume than do traditional florists, they can sell their flowers at a lower cost than your local posh shop. Indeed, more than half of all supermarkets in the country have a floral department, according to the Society of American Florists, and a third of all supermarkets are considered "full-service," meaning they're well equipped to handle your affair.

How much can you save? Calls around the country unearthed surprising savings! Safeway and Whole Foods supermarkets reported that they could make bridal bouquets—including two dozen roses, greenery, and baby's breath—for between $50 and $65, a huge price drop from traditional florists, where prices generally start at about $75 for a rose bouquet. Additionally, Whole Foods encourages brides to take advantage of discounts they can offer for bulk purchases, which give extra incentive to go with bouquets of a single type of flower. For example, if your heart is set on calla lilies, go calla lilies all the way—and they'll make it worth your while.

Who Knew?

New stock generally arrives at supermarkets on the same days each week. Find out when D Day is at the supermarket you're considering using so that you can ensure that you will get the freshest flowers.

Jenny experienced this savings success firsthand. After getting a hideously high quote of $1,500 for her all–calla lily wedding, she decided to head to her local supermarket, the aptly named Price Chopper. Since the supermarket buys wholesale in bulk, they were able to extend the savings to Jenny, making the same flowers and arrangements for $700, less than half the price!

Decide What's Worth Dressing Up

One of the first things that you can do to maximize your budget is to think wisely about exactly where you want and need flowers. Sure, it might be nice to have petals blanketing every square inch of your reception room; a chuppah made of rare, exotic blooms; and personalized bouquets for every single attendee. But come on, shake off the Cinderella fantasy and let's get down to business. Certain elements are essential, and others are essentially unnecessary. The general rule of thumb is to decorate areas that will get the most traffic and draw the most eyes. For instance: Men's room, no; cake table, yes.

A Must

* **The wedding party's bouquets and boutonnieres.** Since these will be in the photos, they definitely will be important. But keep 'em small and simple. After the ceremony and the aisle walk, they'll just get tossed on the table and forgotten.

* **The altar or chuppah decorations.** Beyond the fact that all eyes are directed exactly there, surrounding your "I do's" with lavish flowers infuses the ceremony itself with a beautiful weight. But there's no need to approximate the David Gest/Liza Minnelli's junglelike to-do: Two simple large arrangements on pedestals will offer an arresting frame.

* **The table centerpieces.** Impress your guests where they'll be spending most of their time. They don't need to be towering displays, but some little touches are essential.

A Must Not

- **A petal-strewn aisle.** This fantastical touch doesn't come cheap. Considering you might need 40 to 50 roses per twenty feet, a standard aisle could require petals from 1,000 roses, costing you hundreds of dollars. Most people aren't going to be looking down, so they'll miss this expensive touch anyway. At some venues, a restriction on throwing rice prompts florists to toss in rose petals for the same purpose (for free). Ask and you may receive.

- **The ceremony chairs.** Some folks like to drape flowers across the chairs along the aisle. Believe me, your ceremony will be just as beautiful without the added blooms.

- **The stage.** Your band or DJ's entertainment will duly satisfy the crowds without a lavish display.

- **Every single table.** From the place where you sign the marriage contract or license to the cake table, every square inch of your wedding doesn't need to have its own scheme. You can take it down a notch and still have the same overall visual effect.

Multitasking Flowers

As you shift gears from ceremony to reception, think of wise ways to have your flowers do double-duty. Being a little ingenious can seriously slash your floral budget.

From altar to dance floor. As the focal point shifts from your ceremony to the dance floor, move the floral pedestals as well so that you can buy half as many flowers.

Wedding Chic Word to the Wise:
Very Kind Venues

The place you choose to have the ceremony can drastically affect your floral budget. For example, if you decide to rent out a sleek, minimalist, loftlike raw space, your floral budget can skyrocket because you'll need to give the room an extreme makeover. Alternatively, having your wedding in a fragrant backyard or in a greenhouse can be kind on the eyes—and on the floral budget.

My friend Megan, who works as an editor at *Martha Stewart Living* magazine, got married in St. Paul, Minnesota, where she grew up. I went to her wedding and was simply stunned by how elegantly simple her décor was, thanks in part to a wise venue choice. She and her now-husband decided to have their reception at a historic library downtown, a fitting choice because they are both bibliophiles. Ceiling-high stacks of old books and periodicals and echoey marble floors provided the beautiful backdrop. They didn't need to do all that much to dress up the room. If you swirled around, the masses of colorful book spines could easily have been thousands of dollars' worth of flowers. Anything more would have been unnecessary. Megan's mother rented a few bushy green trees and strung white lights through them. Rather than creating elaborate floral centerpieces, she opted for simple long strands of ferns on the long, wooden library tables, accented with delicate

Continued

baby's breath and votive lights to lend some warmth. The effect was breathtaking—and stunningly low-cost, coming in at less than $250. She did it without a single bloom, thanks to the venue.

Plan wisely at the beginning, and your venue choice can save you thousands of dollars in the end.

From your hands to the table. Instead of forgetting all about your bouquet until the dreaded stress-inducing toss at the end of the night, put all your flowers to use during the ceremony. Place the bouquets on the cake table so that you don't have to dress it up separately.

Beyond Blooms:
Creative Centerpiece Ideas

Who says you need flowers to dress up your tables? Why not think outside the box? Expand your floral repertoire beyond roses, and you'll be able to afford more beautiful flowers for the same money you would have spent on boring blooms. Why take the easy route? Some bright bloom ideas:

- **Go crazy with citrus.** Slice open bright yellow lemons and place them on a platter strewn with complementary petals. The citrus smell will also add a beautiful touch. Citrus fruits can hold up for hours without wilting like more fragile flowers.

- **Think bamboo.** Have fun with feng shui and use some lucky spiraling bamboo shoots in a vase with marbles. A little goes a long way. You can carry it across the altar with you for keeps.

Budget-Friendly Venues, Floral-wise

Botanical gardens
Beaches
Backyards
Libraries
Restaurants

Budget-Busting Venues, Floral-wise

Arty lofts
Civic auditoriums
Military buildings
Drab banquet halls

- **Place a few pinecones around.** At a winter or fall wedding, spray-painted gold pinecones on a platter can create a stunning centerpiece.

- **Opt for food instead of flowers.** Jenny Rinzler, the event manager at Rose & Radish florists in San Francisco, loves to do small clusters of tomatoes or cherries on a table. The bright colors really draw the eye, and fruits and veggies can come a lot cheaper than flowers. She suggests other foodstuff that works well: kumquats, persimmons, pomegranates, cranberries, pears, and apples. Another tasty option is clusters of cascading grapes. Best of all, your boldest guests can dig right in and nosh!

- **Do something berry nice.** Berries can have the same explosive burst of color as flowers, and—depending on the season—a far friendlier price.

• **Substitute petals for elaborate centerpieces.** Depending on the venue, you may not need to go for crazy height. Some bright petals sprinkled across the table with a bowl of floating candles can be equally stunning.

General Cost-Saving Strategies

• **Join forces with other wedding parties happening in your venue.** It always pays to befriend your neighbors, especially when it comes to your floral budget. Find out if there is a wedding before yours on the same day. Either convince the bride before you that your taste is best—or settle on some common ground. (Roses are a universal favorite, of course.) That way, you can actually share arrangements. And not only can you save on flowers, you can also save on delivery fees because you can share the charge.

• **Rent rather than buy.** There's a reason that they call it "disposable income." When it comes to weddings, you can do a lot of disposing. Sure, you can buy an incredible assortment of flowers that you'll toss within days—or you can rent trees, bushes, and other flora from nurseries. You'll need to make a few phone calls to find a store willing to rent in your area, but it's worth your time. Nurseries that rent plants and flowers for weddings generally charge a percentage of the retail value, from 20 to 50 percent, which can soften the budgetary blow on blooms. That means you can get exactly what you might want on loan. For example, at one nursery in Livermore, California, you can rent a $25 blooming rose bush for $6.25. Then you don't need to also plan out who takes what at the end of the night.

- **Be flexible with market buy.** Plan a dinner party months in advance, and you don't necessarily benefit from the freshest fish on sale the day of. The same goes for your wedding flowers. If you hire a florist you trust (which you should be doing anyway), then entrust him or her to buy wisely the morning of your wedding, going for the flowers that are the best prices that day. Work with them ahead of time to create a large list of the blooms you like in general, and that way you can give them options for a market buy. Florists can get flowers that need to move at half the price compared to the hotter commodities. Even if they do a half–market buy, purchasing certain flowers at a discount and combining them with more expensive flowers, they can use the market-buy flowers as lower-cost filler. Flexibility pays.

- **Employ mirrors to enhance small arrangements.** Like a small apartment seemingly enlarged by lots of well-placed mirrors, reflections caused by mirrors under your centerpieces will make small arrangements seem like veritable jungles.

- **Go for a single tone rather than tying together several colors.** If you keep your general color scheme monochromatic, you can create an elegant touch by having bunches of one type of less-pricey bloom, like carnations. Similarly, punch up a thinner red rose bouquet by sprinkling in bright red cranberries. If you try to thread together several colors, you will need to be more adventurous with your selection of flowers—and your price will rise. A single orchid or bird of paradise can carry a bouquet just as well as several sunflowers. They are all beautiful, unconventional ideas. And simplicity stretches your budget. Dana planned on blanketing her wedding site with daisies, which she got from the market just before her wedding. "It's like your house and you're just having a party. Quirky is the way to go, with plain flowers."

• **Minimize the price-raising middlemen: go to a "grower direct."** Scour the Yellow Pages for local florists and start dialing, asking for direct growers. They have their own greenhouses and grow their own flowers, rather than buying them wholesale and charging you an additional percentage on what they paid. The markup on flowers can be as much as 400 percent at regular florists. And that doesn't even include design fees, delivery charges, and anything else they can dream up to add another 10 percent here and there, like

---

Wedding Chic Word to the Wise:
Wholesale Flower Markets

Wholesale markets are to flowers what sample sales are to shopping. At first they seem like an exclusive, foreign concept ("Samples won't fit me! You have to be in the know to find out about them!"). But they're surprisingly more accessible than you might think. Folks who do this for a living often have access well before the novices among us. (For example, the professionals can get the best flowers starting at 2 a.m.) But for those of us who like to rise well—*well*—after 5 a.m., wholesale flower markets are generally accessible to the public after a certain hour. If you find that in your hometown

Continued

they don't let in any laypeople, buddy up to a store-owner whom you know, whether a florist or a boutique owner. Often all it takes is a tax ID number and a business to gain access.

Once you're inside, you'll see what all the fuss is about. The beauty of a supremely discounted flower market or outlet is that you get wholesale prices on flowers. For the intrepid bride who wants to take on the task of doing her own arranging (not as scary as it might seem!), you can save as much as 50 percent by buying flowers at wholesale prices. In some cities, like San Francisco, they make the process even friendlier by having designers on hand to help you plan your centerpieces. Just come well equipped with magazine photos of what you like, and they'll help stock your basket with the right blooms. *Not bad!*

Lynn Harris got great deals on her wedding flowers by going to a wholesaling district. "I'm into flowers and plants, but the corners were so worth cutting; we went to a flower-wholesaling district and cased the joint. We asked what would be in season in November, during our wedding. They said cyclamen and azalea. We picked them up two days before the wedding."

If gaining entry to your local wholesale flower market proves too difficult, there is still another cost-saving option. Try a farmer's market, where you'll be buying flowers directly from the growers, again eliminating price hikes from middlemen.

extra travel costs or flower plumping pre-party. Knock out one of those middlemen, and you can see a dramatic drop in prices.

Timing Is Everything

When you wed is almost as important as *where* you wed, in terms of maximizing your floral budget. Getting married near certain major holidays can bust your floral budget. According to the Society of American Florists, Christmas and Hanukkah represent the number-one and -two flower-giving season. And 57 percent of all cut-flower purchases on Valentine's Day are roses. Where there is demand, suppliers are inclined to hike prices. If you're getting married around any of the holidays below, you'll need to get extra-creative with your flower ideas:

Valentine's Day
Mother's Day
Easter or Passover
Christmas, Hanukkah, or New Year's
Thanksgiving

Season-by-Season Flower Guide

While you might have a serious, unyielding vision for exactly which flowers you want at your wedding (peach tulips as far as the eye can see!), being a little flexible can pay off. Everyone knows that it's a good idea financially to use flowers that are in season, but who among us can deftly recite exactly what is in season when?

In fact, buying out-of-season flowers can cost up to eight times more than what you would spend on local, in-season blooms. It pays to do a little homework. Even if you're working with a florist you trust to know which flowers will be in season at your wedding, it's always good to come armed with your own information. Perhaps there's something he or she didn't consider.

In addition to finding flowers in season, certain flowers can be better priced for your region. Herewith, a general, handy, region-by-region, season-by-season guide (to get a bigger list of blooms, pin down the perfectly priced flowers for your season through the California Commission on Cut Flowers at www.ccfc.org/flowers/flowers.html):

The West

Summer: *delphinium, gardenia, hydrangea, rose, violet*
Fall: *chyrsanthemum, gerbera daisy, hydrangea, lisianthius, pansy, rose*
Winter: *eucalyptus, evergreen, fruit blossoms, tulip*
Spring: *forsythia, iris, lily of the valley, pansy, poppy, ranunculus, rose, tulip*

The East

Summer: *delphinium, hydrangea, rose, sunflower, zinnia*
Fall: *amarayllis, berries, crab apple, hydrangea, rose, sunflower*
Winter: *berries, dried flowers, evergreens*
Spring: *cherry blossom (very early), dogwood, hyacinth, hydrangea, lilac, lily of the valley, peony, tulip*

The Midwest

Summer: *clematis, daisy, garden roses, gladiolus, hydrangea, sunflower, zinnia*

Fall: *berries, crab apple, dahlia, rose, sunflower*
Winter: *berries, dried flowers, evergreens*
Spring: *cherry blossom (very early), daffodil, forsythia, lilac, lily of the valley, peony, tulip*

The South

Summer: *azalea, hydrangea, iris, rose, sunflower, zinnia*
Fall: *galax, hydrangea, rose berries, sassafras, sumac*
Winter: *evergreens, hydrangea, poinsettia, rose*
Spring: *dogwood, forsythia, foxglove, rose, sweet pea, tulip, viburnum, wisteria*

Think Locally

Like produce, certain flowers vary in price in different areas of the country. Of course, if you're set on certain blooms, you can pay up the wazoo for exactly what your heart desires any time of year, thanks to the South American flower market. But it can pay to support local growers. Pam Trotter, a florist in Oklahoma, says that you simply can't beat the price of flowers in California. "The cost of living there is so expensive, and a gallon of milk might be twice what we pay, but flowers are cheap." Trotter buys and ships her flowers from California, hiking prices as much as four times as high. When outfitting a whole venue, this kind of price difference can make or break a bride. This might be something you want to consider when deciding between his hometown in South Dakota and yours in San Diego.

Once you have decided on your date and venue, before selecting your flowers, you can actually research which flowers will get you the best value in your city through the USDA. This government agency updates the cost of wholesale fresh flowers across the country. That means you can find out exactly how much wholesalers are charging your local florist. And if they can get a deal on freesia, so can you. Head to www.ams.usda.gov/fv/mncs/ornterm.htm to get the straight dope about the price your florists are paying for flowers. On a random day in October, here's a sampling of the floral price spread across the country for both gardenias and gerberas:

Gardenia (per bloom)

Philadelphia: $1.50
San Francisco:$2 to $3.25
Boston: $3.75 to $4.50
Chicago: $4 to $5
Seattle: $5.25 to $6

Gerbera (per stem)

San Francisco: $0.65 to $0.75
Philadelphia: $0.80 to $0.85
Boston: $0.85
Chicago: $0.85 to $0.95
Seattle: $1 to $2

Decide on the Most Durable Flowers

While you might think the most important factor in choosing flowers is their look, even the most beautiful blooms won't look so hot if they're drooping before the ceremony is over. If you're getting married in a hot or humid climate, you'll need to be especially mindful about which flowers you choose, but in general, opt for the hardiest flowers to make sure you get the most endurance for your money.

Hardiest Flowers

Carnations
Dahlias
Freesia
Gladiolas
Greenhouse roses
Hypericum (aka Saint-John's-wort)
Lilies
Mums
Orchids
Ranunculus
Sunflowers
Tuberoses
Zinnias

Fragile Flowers

Calla lilies
Daisies
Peonies
Sweet peas

Sure to Fall Before the First Drink

Gardenias
Hydrangeas
Lilacs
Lily of the valley

Stephanotis
Tulips
Wildflowers

The Biggest Blooms
for Your Bucks

Similarly, some flowers will save you lots of money because they're so big that you don't need to buy lots of them. How does this work? The bigger the bloom, the fewer flowers you'll actually need to buy to fill a vase. When it comes to flowers, size does matter. Here's a guide to choosing the biggest blooms.

Biggest, Budget-Friendly Blooms: African marigolds, carnations, dahlias, football mums, gardenias, gladiolas, hydrangeas, spider mums, stargazer lilies, sunflowers.

Smallest, Budget-Busting Blooms: dendrobium orchids, French tulips, forget-me-nots, lily of the valley, mini calla lilies

Buyyourweddingflowersonlineto
savemoney.com

Although many online businesses have gone kaput.com, that doesn't mean there aren't still some great ways to cash in on the new economy. Because Web-based stores have lower overhead (no storefront, and so on), they can often offer some fantastic deals. Leave your anxiety aside and believe that buying your wedding flowers online can be one of your wisest budgetary moves.

My friend Alex, a Web designer, planned one of the most stylish, cost-conscious weddings I've ever heard of. A super-chic girl, she's the type who looks amazing and always has the scoop on sly ways to save money.

When it came to flowers, she and her fiancée opted to use two different websites. "It's nice because the flowers come really fresh and they're not transferred through the middlemen," she explained. They ordered $700 worth of flowers, which arrived by FedEx two days before the event, giving them time to arrange. Alex went to the Chelsea Flower Market to pick up filler flowers, and she ordered vases wholesale through a store where her husband works. Everything went off without a hitch. The flowers arrived on schedule, and they were still perfectly closed, cracking open *just* in time for the wedding.

Good Websites for Buying Your Wedding Flowers

www.theflowerexchange.com
www.flowersbulbs.com
www.matternflwrs.com
www.marisolblooms.com
www.fischerandpage.com
www.2dozenroses.com

How to Arrange Your Own Flowers

*I*f you have decided to scour the Web and search out the best deals on your blooms—or if you picked out the choicest stems at the local wholesale flower market—brava! But your work is only half done. All of the flowers will arrive (fingers crossed) two days before the event. Now it's time to gather your trusty friends and family and put them to work. Here's a sample timeline of what you'll need to do if you have decided to be the expert in Wedding Flower Arranging 101. Take matters into your own well-manicured hands! One wonderful resource to guide you through the possibly thorny process is *The Knot Book of Wedding Flowers.* It will guide you through the complexities of making your own centerpieces and bridal bouquets. Be sure to practice a lot before the big event, especially if you're green at the whole flower biz. Trial runs can truly diminish stress.

To get a sense for how everything can come together seamlessly, here's the savvy schedule of one bride who made thirty centerpieces, four large arrangements, five bridesmaid's bouquets, a bride's bouquet, and twelve corsages—all for $800.

The blooms: roses, lemon leaves, bells of Ireland, curly willow, calla lilies.

The specs: 1,000 red roses ($500), orange and rust calla lilies, green bells of Ireland, lemon leaves and garland, several $4 white porcelain pitchers, and 16 tall rolled-rim glass vases from Pier 1.

Total cost: $800

T-Minus Two Days

Noon: Flowers arrive. Remove from boxes. Place in cool water, cutting greenery that falls below the water line.

Evening: Dethorn all roses. Arrange centerpieces. Mist and cover with small trash liners.

T-Minus One Day

Morning, afternoon, and evening: assemble corsages. Mist and place in resealable bags in the refrigerator.

The Big Day

Morning: assemble bouquets. Pluck petals from extra roses and place in resealable bags to sprinkle on tables and in the aisle. Transport everything to the site.

Candles

Sure, flowers are nice, but a bride can't live and die by blooms alone. Just like a fresh wall color can revive a small apartment, a few candles can completely—and inexpensively—transform the aesthetic of the room, transporting you to a magical place.

When I knew that we had only so much money to devote to our floral budget, I became fixated on sprinkling dozens of candles around the room. I wanted to create the romantic, intimate vibe that only twinkling light can provide. But I was also concerned that we would need to find candles that wouldn't burn out before the dancing began. I figured that we would need at least six hours of burning time.

I have to admit that candles have always been confusing to me. The range from low to luxe is truly vast, and you can either spend a dollar or drop hundreds on a variety of candles. So what's the difference between high-end and low-end? And what could work well for weddings?

Candle Choices

TEALIGHTS

The Look: little, round, and squat; enclosed in aluminum or plastic cups; float nicely in bowls.
The Burn Length: 4 to 5 hours

VOTIVES

The Look: squat and a little taller; group well together in neat glass or plastic containers

The Burn Length: 8 to 12 hours for the best

PILLARS

The Look: thick cylinder; stands alone without a container

The Burn Length: depends on the height, but long enough that you don't have to worry

TAPERS

The Look: long and thin, comfortable at elegant dinners

The Burn Length: depends on the height; figure 30 to 50 minutes per inch

Bright Ideas for Candles

• **Buy wisely for the best deals.** Forget chic upscale houseware stores or having your florist provide them for $5 apiece. When it comes to buying candles for your wedding, you're going for bulk. Head to your local hardware store, Target, or IKEA. You can also stock up online on eBay or websites like www.buyacandle.com. One of my favorite places to buy candles is an all-purpose Chinese housewares shop. Amid the paper curtains and jars of hoisin sauce, you'll find deals like 100 votives for $10. All you'll need are little glass containers that you can generally find for less than $1 apiece. Voilà, you've saved $390 by running one errand rather than delegating it to your florist.

• **Rely on trial and error.** If you're trying a new kind of candle—and you're planning to buy in bulk—then you'll be well served to buy one and see how it works at home. Does it burn faster than you expected? Does the wax drip everywhere? Does it collapse as it gets shorter?

• **Use candles to fill out a thin floral budget.** Candles work wonders in transforming the aesthetic of your space. Place them in odd numbers around your centerpieces. Put on any mantle, and line them up around the cake table.

• **For an added bonus, buy scented candles.** I recently attended my friend Emily's wedding in suburban Detroit. She had positively blanketed the banquet room of a ritzy hotel in creamy vanilla pillar candles. Everywhere you went, the scent enveloped you—and the effect was supremely luxurious. At the end of the night, guests were invited to take candles with them. To give you a sense of how long a pillar can last, Michael and I still have the vanilla candle, a beautiful memento from Emily's wedding, on a dresser in our bedroom a full year later. I consider that the sweet smell of success.

The Contract Basics

Before signing, make sure the following points are addressed in your floral contract:

• The date, time, and address of the event.

• The name of and contact info for the florist.

• All the details of your order, including the number of bouquets, the types of flowers to be used, and the accessories (or, if you plan to have your florist do a season-specific market buy, be sure that is written into the contract).

• The specifics of delivery (who will be delivering, how far in advance of the event the flowers will be delivered, who will be setting up the flowers).

• A specific outline of the fees (including a breakdown of all costs).

• The deposit due date, and balance due date.

• The florist's cancellation and refund policy.

The Bottom Line

• Learn the most important traits in a florist—beyond their fresh stock.

• Scope out supermarkets for great deals.

• Decide what's worth dressing up.

• Make your flowers multitask.

• Consider some creative and cost-effective centerpiece ideas.

• Try to find a local wholesale market for great prices.

• Bone up on what's in season when and where so you can go local.

- Choose the most durable, long-lasting blooms.

- Buyyourflowersonlinetogetsuperprices.com.

- Further dress up the room in the most cost-effective way with candles.

8 · The Photos:

Make Saving on Your Photographer a Real Snap

*M*y friend Jane had a wonderfully *Wedding Chic* affair when she and her now-husband, Martin, got married last summer. Because Jane grew up in New Orleans, it felt like the natural choice for the New York City–based couple to head south for their wedding. The jewelry designer for Linea Nervenkitt, Jane is a whiz at being thrifty while also being stylish. And as a neuroscience Ph.D. candidate at Harvard, she also applied a scientific zeal to scoring the best deals for her wedding. Although they managed to pull off a miracle of a wedding for practically pennies, she had one major regret: having a friend snap shots instead of hiring a professional photographer. After returning to New York, we were heading to dinner one night when she sighed to me, "I wish we'd spent *more* money on the photographer. I'm not happy with the photos." It's true—if there's one place to invest, it's here. It might not seem like such a high priority while you're in the whirl of anticipation, but photos are one aspect you're likely to regret scrimping on later.

Find the Most Fab Photographer

*M*y friend Alex studied photography at the School of Visual Arts in New York City. So when it came time to line up a photographer for her New Jersey wedding, she knew exactly what she wanted. In a great twist, a former classmate volunteered to do double-duty as both guest and wedding photographer. She paid for all his costs, from supplies to film and printing. She was able to feel confident that she was getting exactly what she wanted and that the photos would be beautiful.

But not everyone has arty pals who can step in and snap your wedding for you. It's not like you want to entrust a third cousin with such a monumental task as documenting one of the most significant life events you'll ever experience. What happens if he starts to booze it up and everything gets a wee bit blurry midway through the reception? Lasting memories of your wedding are not something to gamble on. Leave this business to folks who make a living doing it. That said, if you're lucky enough to have a friend who is professional or semiprofessional (and you love their work), by all means take them up on an offer to photograph your wedding.

Indeed, photography is one of the few areas where you actually want to use the *W* word and find someone who specializes in weddings. Why? Most important, trust. You really don't have insurance with photographers. They have one chance to take these critical pictures. If the photos don't turn out, it's not like you can restage your wedding. So you need to find someone whom you can completely trust to capture the event, someone who has done this before.

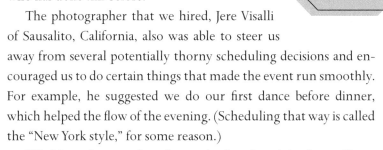

The photographer that we hired, Jere Visalli of Sausalito, California, also was able to steer us away from several potentially thorny scheduling decisions and encouraged us to do certain things that made the event run smoothly. For example, he suggested we do our first dance before dinner, which helped the flow of the evening. (Scheduling that way is called the "New York style," for some reason.)

"Wedding photographers know the flow," explains Laura Plageman, a wedding photographer in Oakland, California. "There's a predictable sort of routine in most weddings. And we have the ability to work with a lot of different kinds of people and deal with challenging situations." In fact, managing to get divorced stepparents and dueling half-siblings in the same shot—speedily, smoothly, and beautifully—before the ceremony is a mighty talent worth shelling out the bucks for.

If you are trying to save a penny and decide to opt for a fashion photographer, beware! You could find yourself working with a photographer who fancies himself "on location" for *Vogue* or some such glam glossy, jumping all over the pews, trying to get shots. "Yeah, I love it! I love you! Give me some lip! Be pouty! Fabulous, dahhling! Faaabulous!"

How do you find the best wedding photographer for you? Here's what not to do: pick up the phone book, choose the biggest advertisement, and call, saying you want a wedding photographer. (The subtext: "Overcharge me! I'm a sucker.")

Instead, be the informed super-smart and savvy consumer you are. Even if you can't gather any good recommendations from friends (which is always the best place to start), there's hope! Finding pros in any field is as simple as knowing where to gather information. Just turn to some reputable organizations, such as the following groups, and put together a list of contenders:

• Professional Photographers of America (PPA) maintains a database of thousands of wedding photographers. (Contact them at www.ppa.com; 800-786-6277.)

• The Wedding Photojournalist Association (WPJA) requires members to apply and pass rigorous scrutiny. Fewer than half are accepted, so you can expect la crème de la crème of shutterbugs. (Find them at www.wpja.org.)

Two Different Styles of Photography

*I*n order to be the most informed consumer, you must learn to speak *la lingua* so you'll know what you should ask. Consider this your photography crib sheet. Basically, there are two different styles of wedding photography: classic and photojournalistic. To break it down: Your mom will want classic, and you might pine for a little of-the-moment, candid, behind-the-scenes shots, the moments you didn't happen to catch with your own two misty eyes at the time.

When it comes to the portraits, a classic wedding photographer is a pro at getting Every, Single, Permutation of your family and your honey's in posed shots. Now . . . the sisters! Now . . . all the aunts! Now . . . everyone who is 5'4"! And then for the relaxed shots, they'll script some moment like the bridesmaids doing a little flirty number showing a little leg, the grooms-men slapping the groom on the back in a jokingly ominous way ("Don't go through with it, man!"). Our photographer discreetly came and asked us at one point if we could steal away a few minutes to take some portraits of just the two of us, mid-reception. The photos he took then are some of my absolute favorites. Our faces ooze joy.

Alternatively, a photographer who does more of the photojournalistic style excels at capturing the little moments, the candid shots. The downside is that you may find out later that—geez, there is no record of your uncle being at the event—but you'll have to decide when you choose a photographer how important that is to you (or to your parents!). David Roberts, the founder of the Wedding Photojournalist Association, says that photojournalists are a good choice because they're more flexible if something, God forbid, goes awry. "They're forced to go into situations where lighting is horrible, subjects are difficult to work with. . . . A lot of people could go into the situation and say, 'There's no picture here,'" he explains. "We can make a good picture anywhere. I have that confidence."

What did I choose? We had both—in one person! The photographer we hired had an assistant who snapped black-and-white candids while he was setting up the stiffer shots. I didn't want a whole album of canned smiles that give themselves away thanks to unsmiling eyes. There's nothing worse than pictures of freaked-out brides with fake, shrill-looking smiles pasted on. Yikes!

We were able to get two in one, the best of both worlds. A photographer's assistant is actually a worthwhile expense as well. And don't worry, you're not the one who should be required to shoulder it; your photographer should factor it into his fee. Find out if the photographer you hire will have an assistant. It costs the photographer about a few hundred dollars, because the assistant is often working as an apprentice with the established honcho. And just as we experienced, the assistant's photographs worked to complement the main photographer's more polished work. Together the two of them made a great package.

Digital vs. Film

One of the things you will want to ask a prospective photographer before plunking down the plastic and signing on the dotted line is whether he'll be shooting in film or digital—or both. Unless you're a shutterbug, here's the scoop on what that difference will mean to you, thanks to Denis Reggie, the wedding photographer of more than twenty Kennedy weddings, including that of JFK Jr. and Carolyn Bessette.

"Digital means the freedom to shoot a lot more photographs, so you don't have to reload as often," he explained. "Last Friday we did over five thousand images over the weekend; one thousand two hundred on Friday during the walk-through, and three thousand eight hundred during the wedding. We now have a wonderful

Wedding Chic Word to the Wise:
Getting a CD Made

One great advantage to having your photographer shoot digitally is that he or she can give you a CD of all the images. You'll need to negotiate this from the beginning, but your options could include: a digital contact sheet; a hard-copy contact sheet with all the images on it (these can also be done with film); or a CD with the images, which you can take anywhere to have printed. Getting a CD is great because you can make multiple copies of it. But having a CD doesn't mean that you can reprint from the images. Your photographer may own the copyright and only give you low-resolution versions of the pictures, which won't print as well as the high-resolution versions he holds on to. Whatever you do, negotiate at the outset what you will retain and what your photographer will retain.

chance to carefully review the material with the eye of a historian looking to document the event in real time. . . . This journalistic edge brings with it a need for deeper coverage; we're looking for the little things." (Although digital works best, as Reggie explains, for the photojournalistic touches, you might want your photographer to use film for the portraits, as the resolution will be crisper.)

Except for the initial cost of the equipment, digital is also cheaper. With digital photography, you have the ability to have your wedding covered in greater depth without necessarily elevating the cost, says Reggie. "In the film world, three thousand photographs

Wedding Chic Word to the Wise: The Value of Good Vibes

I knew the minute I laid my eyes on him that we were meant to be. Jere emitted a suave, easy, and friendly vibe. He listened, he watched, and I was sold. Choosing your wedding photographer is about more than just finding who has the best package. It's also about so much more than the merits of the photog's album.

My friends Lisa and Josh said the photographer at their wedding drove them crazy with his demands for all the shots *he* had to get. It was more about him crossing shots off his list than helping them enjoy their own event. Sweaty and pushy, he kept dragging them away from the party.

Not so with our photographer. Jere operated behind the scenes amazingly well. Only after the event, when I looked at all of the photos, did I realize just how much he caught—including our private moment just after the ceremony on a side deck. At first I was a little creeped out (did this guy have cameras planted in all corners of the joint?), but it was actually quite sweet that he was able to capture our secret "Ohmygodican'tbelieve-we'reactuallymarried" moment without us even realizing it. Those are some of my favorite shots now, because they are completely candid and rife with emotion.

would be thousands of dollars in cost. That's not true for digital."
That's because you only print the photos you want.

Photog Red Flags

efore we found the photographer we fell in love with, there
was a cast of other, less appealing applicants. One notable
photographer I visited was obsessed with the intricate shadow work
in her book. Her zeal scared
me, mostly because I thought
she fancied herself a faaah-
bulous fashion photographer,
not a wedding photographer.
Clearly, she still considered
herself an artiste—not a service provider. While I'm all
for beautiful photography, it
was important for me to limit
the number of borderline-
cheesy shots (A pic of my
feet! A pic of my hands! A pic

> ## Who Knew?
>
> If your photographer tells you that it will cost you extra to have some black-and-white photos mixed in with your colors, here's what you should say: "Thanks! Buh-bye." Black-and-white film and photographs shouldn't cost significantly more to buy or to develop than color, so beware of the photographer who considers them another opportunity to tack on a sneaky surcharge.

of shadow work on the groom's thigh!). I wanted to make sure
we'd come away with the bare bones of what was important. Also,
I didn't want to pay fashion-world rates for my wedding photographer.

"There are so many different terms that people throw out," agrees
David Roberts, of the Wedding Photojournalist Association. "The bot-
tom line is that you should look at their work and think, *Do I like this?*
If you look at it and think, *I could do this myself,* don't hire them."

Here's a sampling of some smoke and mirrors that a photographer might use to sell you on his or her higher-priced artiste skills.
Beware the unnecessary extras!

- **Sepia tones.** This old-worldy aesthetic, slight color added to black-and-white photos, says one of two things: grandma back in her days in the tenement building or wild, wild West bordello shots. Neither of these things is what you're shooting for with your wedding photos. Plus, while the effect can be snazzy, it also often carries a price hike, as many photographers consider it a luxury touch. Tread simply with your wedding photography. There's no need to run circles around your wedding photographs, dressing them up with superstar touches. Your beautiful happy faces will have enough of an effect on their own.

Who Knew?

In a list of the ten most overpaid professions, *CBS Marketwatch* on November 6, 2003, listed wedding photographers as number ten, noting that "many charge $2,500 to $5,000 for a one-day shoot, client meeting and processing time that runs up to 20 hours or more, and the cost of materials." Not bad for about twenty hours' worth of work. Sure, they sometimes need to fend off ballistic brides, but that seems like a small price for $250 an hour!

- **Split frames.** This tricky technique requires a special filter in the camera—or digital re-creation after the fact, which can cost as much as $150 an hour. That doesn't sound so pretty, does it?

- **Touch-ups.** Unless you plan to publish your wedding photos on the cover of *Glamour*, you don't really want to pay your photographer to remove all traces of the pores on your nose. Vanity has its limits, my friend. No one looks absolutely perfect at all times, so don't expect creamy skin, an impeccable smile, your dress to hang just so, and—oh, yeah—your husband to be equally on at all moments. Correcting "errors" in the photos will run you hundreds of extra dollars—an hour. Consider your flaws simply part of being human—even on this, the most unique of days.

How Long Is Long Enough?

The truth of the matter is, no matter how much you like whomever you hire, you don't want them there till the bitter end to capture your weepy lovey-dovey moments with your best friend from grade school ("I can't believe I'm getting married! Do you remember that sleepover . . . !?"). Nope. Save that one for the virtual memory. There are things you just won't want documented. There's also a limit to how many hours you really need your photographer to be there.

Ultimately, you only need three to four hours to achieve a wonderfully rich shot list. Laura, from Hawaii, took this to the extreme, scheduling the cake cutting before the first course of dinner so that the photographer didn't have to twiddle his thumbs during three full courses. He could just take off after the cake. Now that's a savvy bride.

Certainly, Laura's cost-saving scheduling might seem like a wise financial move in some ways, but you'll have to think it over for yourself. After all, you don't want to sacrifice the feeling of the affair for the sake of the photos. Do things in the order that you'll enjoy them the most. All things considered, however, you truly won't need a photographer for more than three or four hours, including the ceremony and the reception. That's plenty of time for the photographer to complete his work.

Savvy Cost-Saving Shot Lists

*I*n order to keep things snappy, photograph-wise, it's best to come prepared with a list of shots you want. Sure, everyone wants a private one-on-one, cheek-to-cheek photo with the bride,

---

Wedding Chic Word to the Wise:
Put a Cap on Portraits

Don't listen to your mother, who would be happy having the photographer use all his time taking formal family portraits. Keep in mind that the total number of portraits should make up only 5 percent of all your shots. Can you think of a more boring set of photographs to look at? Portraits of all permutations of both extended families could be mug shots, as far as I'm concerned. They document who came and what they wore—and everyone has the same stiff smile. Yawn. The guest book has the same ultimate effect. (Uncle Marty? Yup, he was there. Great-aunt Marie? In the house.) I'd rather see a shot of Grandpa and Grandma exchanging a proud peck after the ceremony. Don't let the formal shots overwhelm the total photography package. Keep it quick and simple. Have your photographer spend his time—and your money—focusing on the photos that will resonate the most with you and your husband for years to come.

but for the sake of saving your smile muscles—and your budget—it's important to pare down your shot list to the absolute essentials. Go online to a wedding website such as The Knot (www.theknot .com) to get complete wedding shot lists, and decide which ones are truly important to you. Write down a list (photocopy and hand off to a few people in case one gets misplaced!) and pass it to the photographer to make sure you'll get what you want. In the meantime, consider the following list a starting point for making decisions about which shots are absolutely essential and which are easily missed:

A Go

Portraits
Ceremony shots
Candids, candids, candids (viewing the photos, you'll be transported to the experience of your wedding day)

Forgo

Shots of the bride getting ready
Arty shots of people's feet
Shots of the bride and groom at every single table in the room (boring!)
Toasts (so undynamic!)
Dancing moves (inevitably embarrassing for all involved parties)
Anything involving eating (not pretty)

Decoding the Package Deal

When you sit down with a photographer, after having you *ooh* and *ahh* over plush leather albums of the Greatest Hits of Weddings of Yore, he or she will put down a price sheet that is sure to cause some confusion. Some packages will have a certain number of prints included, and others will have you pay as you go. There are others that will include albums for Mom and Dad, and special extras like photo wedding favors. It can be a little dizzying to try to crunch all the numbers in your head. The one thing you should be wary of is simply opting for the cheapest option. At the end of the day, you could spend a lot more money. That's because, after the day is done, the photographer could entice you to buy all sorts of extra shots once you're feeling nostalgic. Think of it like cell-phone charges. Sure, it's cheap when your minutes are included, but if you go over, you end up paying far more than you could ever have imagined. Buying extra prints from a wedding photographer can easily counteract wise money-saving moves you made earlier in the process, so try to be as realistic with yourself as possible about what you think you'll want in the end. Remember, this is not a high-school yearbook you'll look at maybe five times, tops, in the course of your life. This is an album that your children will be giggling at twenty years from now. ("I can't believe Mom's hair really looked like that!") All that could be included (in addition to a traditional wedding album):

Engagement photos
Parents' albums
Save-the-date shots (photos you can send out as your "save the date" notice invitations)
Polaroids of all arriving guests, to be given to them as favors

In a classic arrangement, at the end of the day, besides whatever extras you end up ordering, your photographer should provide you with contact sheets or proofs (which you could, ideally, keep). After you select from the proofs or contact sheets, the photographer can prepare the album.

General Money-Saving Strategies

• **Negotiate to buy your negatives.** There's positively no better way to save on your photo budget than by getting your hands on your negatives. Most photographers will want to hold on to them—for good reason. Everytime you, or anyone in your family, want a print, the photographer can charge you through the nose. Before assuming that's just the way it has to be, consider asking if you can purchase your negatives. Many brides have found photographers willing to sell the negatives for 10 percent of the total price of the package. It might seem like a lot, but it's worth it. You'll have to do the math about how many prints you'll want and see just how much you can save—but chances are, it's worth it. Some photographers will want to hold on to the negatives for a year, and then they will offer to sell them to you at that point. Factor in shelling out 10 percent.

• **Please yourself with penny-wise printing.** Even if you can't get your hands on the negatives, you're not doomed to overpay for your prints. If your photographer sends you proofs to select the images that you want printed, which ours did, you can actually take those in to have prints made out of them. Spectra Photo Digital in New York City, a lab that many wedding photographers actually use, can print from proofs at a much lower rate than your professional photographer would charge from the negatives. The higher price charged for printing from proofs is still lower than what a wedding photographer will charge a bride for prints from negatives. For example, consider that most wedding photographers charge about $7 and up for 4-by-6 or 5-by-5 reprints. A high-end photo lab might charge more like $5 for a 5-by-5 from proofs. Even if your photographer has included a seal on the prints to prevent duplication, the lab can most likely retouch it out. Whatever you do, however, don't be a total scrooge and scrimp in the wrong way, taking your negatives or proofs to a McPhoto Lab—a shady joint in a mall or a superstore. They can mess up the negative, which you can't do anything about. If you're going to save on the reprint costs by doing it yourself, at least splurge on where you take them to be super-safe.

Who Knew?

"Artistry only" packages, where photographers come in and shoot your wedding for a lower price and give you the negatives to make your own prints, are a great alternative for truly cost-conscious couples.

Make Your Own Amazing DIY Albums

If you're among the lucky few with professional photographer friends—or if you've found a photographer who was willing to sell you the negatives so you can make your own album—the next step is for you to find an appropriately beautiful framework for your photos. You're not going to toss the shots in a shoebox and store it under your bed. Unless you're the kind of girl who has a knack for scrapbooking (sadly, I'm not one), this will be new territory. But it's not as daunting as it might seem when you first walk into a 40,000-square-foot store filled with photo corners and special kinds of glue. Here are the basics you'll need to get started:

1. **The album.** Your first step will be to purchase the right album. Leather is always nice, but that can set you back up to several hundred dollars. One great company with affordable, beautiful albums is Kolo. You'll have no problem finding an elegant product for less than $100. You can find Kolo products at The Art Store, Bed Bath & Beyond, and Per Annum (www.perannum.com). If you'd like to buy professional-quality albums, like Renaissance, head to www.proweddingalbums.com and order  it yourself, rather than through your photographer, and it will save you professional markup that can cost four times the wholesale price. Some of these albums can cost as much as $1,000—so getting a discount is no small affair in terms of savings. Another great resource for wedding albums is Exposures, a catalog and website, at www.exposuresonline.com.

2. **Archival paper.** If you want your grandchildren to be able to pore over your photos, you had better buy the best paper to preserve them. That would be acid-free archival paper, which is pH balanced, meaning it's not going to turn yellow over time. (Remember how the older generation's albums are all slightly yellow-looking now? That's not what we're going for here.)

202 • Wedding Chic

3. **A calculator.** You're not going to be able to include every photograph, and before you slap down your credit card and purchase an album, you need to map out exactly how many photos you plan to include and how you'd like them to appear (i.e., two 3-by-5s on this page, and then a vertical 5-by-7 on the facing page, etc.). This will determine how many pages you'll need to order. Once you put in your order, it's hard to go back and add pages, so always err on the side of overdoing it. There will always be another picture you can put in at the end.

Disposable Cameras: Don't Do It!

*E*veryone starts planning their photography by thinking that scattering disposable cameras around the room is a fantastic idea. But you might want to think twice. If you've ever done it before at dinner parties, you'll remember that one of two things generally happens:

1. A really inappropriate or intoxicated friend decides to hijack a camera and take it to the bathroom, or some such location, capturing moments you'd rather not know happened.

2. One or two enthusiastic friends just take pictures of each other *all* night. While you certainly love your pals, you don't love them enough to merit twenty-four exposures of them grinning with their heads bobbing inward at an angle. Cheese. Or more like Cheesy!

Truly, the disposable camera thing is only for those who have disposable cash. Although it might seem like a low-budget option for photography, if you just have the professional shoot the straight stuff and leave it up to your friends to capture the small moments, your yield will be disappointingly low. Yes, you might get a few worthy shots (especially if you assign a talented, reliable friend to man a camera all night), but you'll spend wads of extra money developing that film to get a few shots of mediocre quality. Verdict: not worth it.

Videography

For some folks, photos just don't cut it. They want to relive the event, pop in a videotape, and sit through the whole shebang all over again (from the sweaty exchange of rings down to the boozy, bitter end). I wasn't one of those people, as I just couldn't imagine watching the video. I'd rather preserve the memory in my good old head. (Contrary to my hunch about the fact that people don't actually watch their videos, the girls I asked actually did, and far more frequently than I suspected: an average of three times each!)

Clea Simon, a Boston-based journalist and author who has written about videography, agrees that it is an unnecessary extra for many. "I'd rather look at one artistic photo than hours of video any day," she says, adding that video is most valuable for folks with a sick or elderly relative who cannot attend the wedding.

Still, about half of all brides opt to get a video of the event made—and that number is actually on the rise. If your budget per-

Who Knew?

Round up folks looking for training in the video arts to do your wedding video. Dana, a friend in Boston, would have loved to have a video of her wedding, but she didn't want to spend the money. She found a classified ad on a wedding message board for a local videographer who was looking to hone his craft. It worked out well for both parties. "The guy now works for PBS and we have a video from a PBS documentarian of our wedding!" she said.

mits, and you're set on videotaping the event for posterity, you should at least do it well—and wisely. Here's how:

- **Get an all-inclusive package.** Make sure that your package includes filming during the ceremony and the reception, interviews with members of the wedding party and family, and editing (allowing your input).

- **Don't be scared by the price.** Informal surveys by Wedding and Event Videographers Association (WEVA) International show that though prices can rise as high as $10,000 and up, you can get a video made for as low as about $1,000.

- **Get the lowdown on lighting.** Find out if your videographer plans to use natural light or blast the room with artificial bulbs. While you want the video to be well lit, you don't want it to seem like you're shooting a movie.

- **Find out the scoop on sound.** "Our ceremony was outside, and sometimes when the wind picked up we couldn't hear the words," recalls one bride. Some videographers choose to mic the bride, groom, and officiant. Be sure to ask what your videographer's strategy is. You don't want to be in the position of getting the sound up full-blast just to hear the I Do's. "I *what*?"

The Best Photographic Gift

y friend Jenn, who is one of the most wonderfully crafty people I know, gave me and Michael one of our best wedding gifts: the gift of photography. Jenn offered to do a Polaroid scrapbook of everyone at the event, which would make up a visual guest book. Over the course of the evening, Jenn snapped candid and posed shots of friends (some individually, and others in unlikely pairings . . .). Then the folks in each photo wrote a message to us next to their names.

Some photographers offer this as an extra option in a package, but shooting Polaroids of all the guests over the course of the night as Jenn did it worked much better, because she shot over a long span of time. People were much looser, and they were excited to swing to the corner of the room where Jenn was stationed and stand for their shot, rather than being herded in like chattel, stiffly at the beginning.

When we looked at the beautiful book a few weeks later, I was immediately, completely transported back to the event by joyful, emotive photos of all our friends and family. Jenn even got a shot of our string trio; it took me a while to figure out that they weren't just distant relatives of Michael's whom I couldn't place!

The Contract Basics

Before signing, make sure the following points are addressed in your contract:

• The date, time, and address of your event.

• The name and contact info for the photographer who will be working the event, as well as the name of his assistant (if any).

- The number of hours you will be hiring the photographer for (including how far in advance of the event the photographer will arrive).

- The hourly fee for overtime charges.

- A specific outline of all fees (including a breakdown of costs—i.e., for proofs, album packages, reprint fees, etc.).

- Your film preference (black-and-white or color).

- Who will keep the negatives.

- The deposit due date and balance due date.

- The photographer's cancellation and refund policy.

The Bottom Line

- Assemble a short list of talented pros in your area by contacting reputable organizations and sources.

- Keep your eyes open for certain obvious red flags when deciding among potential photographers.

- Decide whether you prefer more candid or posed shots—photojournalistic or classic style.

- Consider digital photography, which allows greater flexibility and can be much cheaper.

- Set a reasonable time limit for how long you'll need your photographer to be there.

- Formulate a savvy, cost-saving shot list.

- Learn how to decode a package deal.

- Try to get the rights to your negatives.

- Make your own albums to save big.

- Decide if a video is worth it for you—or your aging relatives.

9 · The Eats:

Create a Wedding Menu with Tastes and Prices You'll Find Palatable

From the colors of the flowers to the type of music to where you want to buy your wedding dress, you have at least some vague idea about what you want. Pink! Funk! Trunk show! But when it comes to the food you will have served at your wedding, somehow you draw a blank. Err . . . chicken or fish? When it comes to wedding food, there's a reason the feast is generally made up of either fish or fowl. Those basic options tend to appease the hungry masses.

Before you start getting into a tizzy about all the dietary preferences of your attendees (Sharon is a vegan! Sandy is kosher vegetarian! Tim's on Atkins!), take a moment to be at peace with one fact: You will never be able to please everyone with your menu. And pleasing everyone shouldn't be your goal. The idea is to provide delicious food that will please most of the people. And, most of all, you.

At the beginning stages of assembling the ingredients for your nuptial feast, it's critical to come to terms with one wonderfully welcome fact: People don't go to weddings simply to dine. So you must not get all whipped up into a froth about which variety of bitter greens you want to serve, whether your game hens are farm-raised, or what your jus will be infused with. Sure, tasty food is important, but it's not like you need to feel compelled to fly in Alain Ducasse to whip up the crème de la crème of wedding meals. "The last thing that anyone remembers at a wedding is food," notes Sheryl Julian, the food editor at the *Boston Globe* and author of *The Way We Cook.*

So it's time to put down the *Gourmet* magazine, turn off the Food Network, stop surfing Epicurious.com, and start planning the most reasonable, affordable, and wonderfully delicious menu possible.

Timing Your Event Wisely

*J*ust like the amount you have to spend to rent your venue, your catering costs will vary significantly, depending on when you choose to schedule your celebration. A brunch menu is going to require far less food than a sit-down dinner. Passed appetizers at a late-afternoon wedding will be significantly more budget-friendly than a ten-station cornucopia buffet dinner.

Around the clock, here's a sense of what kind of food you would need to supply at differently timed events. Note that the later in the day you go, the more you will need to spend on food.

Before 10 a.m.: Sure, you'd only need to provide breakfast food, but don't even think about it! No one should even be awake at this time, much less paying witness to I do's. Save your pennies elsewhere.

10 a.m. to 1 p.m.: Brunch. The budget-friendliest of them all. But somehow, this still comes off as chintzy.

1 p.m. to 4 p.m.: Lunch. This can be a lovely and affordable choice, because you'll also keep your alcohol costs down.

3 p.m. to 7 p.m.: Passed appetizers. If you time it perfectly between lunch and sundown, this can be a sneaky way to avoid paying for a sit-down dinner. Be sure to include coy wording (something like a "late-afternoon celebration") on your invite, however, so your guests will come prepared with half-full stomachs.

7 p.m. onward: any event going past 7 p.m. absolutely requires dinner—the classic, and most costly, wedding option.

Creative Caterers

*I*f you flip open the Yellow Pages and draw a big red circle around Elite Caterers for Your Hoity-Toity Feast, you won't exactly set yourself up for the best, brightest, and most budget-friendly menu. Indeed, you must be mindful about where you find your caterer, because the costs vary widely.

My friend Alex opted to hire friends of friends to cater her wedding. Her husband's boss, who runs a boutique in New York City, uses a set of caterers for all the parties he throws. Alex was able to talk frankly with them about their budget and arrange for a reasonably priced menu and get essentially wholesale prices on the catering costs. Caterers can be your allies in cutting costs; be frank with them from the outset about your budget, and they can work with you to shave a little here, trim the fat there.

Hiring friends of friends is always the best route, but if you're

getting married halfway across the country and are drawing a blank in your mental Rolodex about who might be able to come to your rescue, you do have other options. If at this point you have one vendor you trust, whether it's the photographer, the band, or the florist, ask for the straight dope on their favorite caterer. People in the industry know one another and can recommend their favorites. (Of course, your

venue may require you to use one caterer in particular, in which case, your cost-saving choices will depend on the food they serve.)

Another great place to score a caterer is through your local culinary school. Not every culinary school offers catering, so you'll have to call around. But working the phones is worth it; the prices can be mighty savory when you find a school that does. For example, the California Culinary Academy in San Francisco generally caters about four to five weddings a year, and they charge an extremely reasonable rate, starting at just north of $40 a head—quite a bargain in the pricey Bay Area. And the Johnson and Wales Inn in Seekonk, Massachusetts, charges one-third to one-fourth less than venues just down the road. To find out if there's a catering school near you, check out www.culinaryschools.com.

If you do happen to find a school that doesn't do weddings, don't lose hope. Remember, the *Wedding Chic* bride is nothing if not persistent. Check the bulletin boards to see if any hungry students are looking for catering gigs. Or better yet, suggests Tara Duggan, a food writer for the *San Francisco Chronicle*, post a request yourself. Wanted: One Fab Caterer to Fill Very Important Bellies.

Sit-Down vs. Buffet

our gut instinct might tell you to forgo the sit-down meal for a cheaper buffet to save a bundle. Right? Not necessarily! In a knotty twist of the wedding industry, a postnuptial buffet can actually be more expensive than a sit-down affair. It all comes down to one hard-and-fast fact: choices cost.

If you offer a cornucopia of food options at ten stations around a room, your caterer will have to buy much more food than if you were able to tell her to plan on serving 120 people, each eating the same two things. Yes, a sit-down dinner will require you to hire more servers than will a buffet, but the cost can quickly counteract itself.

Who Knew?

While a big buffet might be a surprising budget-buster, you still have yet another option to the sit-down dinner. Why not have food served family-style? What's more of an ice-breaker than newly acquainted tablemates serving one another dollops of steaming food?

To figure out what's best for you, follow the loose guidelines of Barbara Howard, a wedding consultant in the Metro Detroit area. "A two-meat buffet is more affordable than plated services because you can cut down by half the number of servers. And three- to four-meat buffets are more money than plated service." Got it? Grab your calculator!

Planning a Money-Saving Menu

Once you've settled on the who and the when, you need to square away the what. What will you be serving? Like your flower choices, it will pay off to be somewhat flexible around the date of the event. If you let your caterer have the option to buy what's in season, what looks good, or what's on sale, you can assemble a menu with fresher and more affordably priced ingredients.

Amanda Hesser, a food writer for *The New York Times* and author of *Cooking for Mr. Latte*, did just that. "We just talked in general about possibilities and ideas, with the understanding that the week before the wedding he could change his mind. Say the corn might not be as good as he expected, so we would do something with tomatoes." Flexibility can allow for better ingredients, but it can also allow your caterer to use the allotted budget for more of the good stuff. If you're dead set on artichokes, you might force your caterer into spending a large percentage of his allotted budget on an out-of-season ingredient.

That said, there are certain ingredients that will always be financial red flags, whatever the season. "Anything with foie gras is insane," concludes Sheryl Julian of the *Boston Globe*. But that's only the beginning. There's plenty more insanity. When in doubt, avoid putting these items on your wedding menu. Remember, you have the rest of your life to enjoy these foods, when you're not paying for 100-odd others to shovel it in absentmindedly while flirting with your college roommate.

Financial Red-Flag Foods

Abalone
Ahi tuna
Asparagus
Caviar
Chilean sea bass
Fillet of sole
Foie gras
Lamb
Lobster
Prawns
Raspberries
Risotto
Swordfish
Tenderloin
Veal

Seamless Substitutions

While of course it would be nice to offer a menu filled with foie gras, imported haricots verts drizzled in truffle oil, and fresh lobster, that's not necessarily the wisest way to allocate your funds. "The minute the menu starts with 'made with wild mushrooms, farmed that, wild that, individually braised this, striped that,' the price just keeps going up," Julian instructs.

Forgo the fancy touches and keep things simple. The fact is, any caterer worth his salt will just do a better job feeding the masses with fresh ingredients cooked simply and well as opposed to drizzling everything in a cognac-and-caviar reduction.

However, simplicity doesn't mean you need to resign yourself to boiled chicken and steamed brussels sprouts for your nuptial feast.

Consider each wild menu item an opportunity to slip in a sneaky, lower-cost alternative. No one will know! Or if they do, it's not like they're going to come up and tap you on the shoulder and say, "Hey, where are the soft-shell crabs??" Consider the possible substitutions on the following page—and calculate just how much you could save.

General Strategies

While substitutions are quick ways to save money on your catering costs, you do have some general culinary choices that will also help the cause. Why not try one of these tasty strategies when planning your menu?

- **Eat ethnic.** When Carolyn Jung, the food editor at the *San Jose Mercury News*, was planning her wedding menu, she felt the pressure. "Because of my job, I had to have great food," she explains. But with a cap on the budget, the pressure mounted even more. Her solution? A Chinese banquet, where she served her guests ten courses for the price of one entrée. The wedding menu included crab claws, prawns, and scallops sautéed with fresh greens, filet mignon tenders, and honey-glazed Chilean sea bass (all no-no's if you consult the list opposite, though they did substitute scallop soup for shark-fin soup and crispy chicken for duck). But the whole meal went down easy, costing less than $45 a person. How? She and her husband chose the nicest dim sum palace in San Francisco to hold their ethnic banquet. Other budget-friendly ethnic foods include: Greek, Mexican, Middle Eastern, and Moroccan. "I've known people who've had their favorite taqueria come and do tacos," recalls the *San Francisco Chronicle*'s Tara Duggan.

INSTEAD OF	OPT FOR	SAVE (AVERAGE PERCENTAGES)
Fish and Meat		
Crab cakes	Cheese tartlets	15
Roasted portobello mushrooms	Grilled chicken	10–20
Filet mignon	Flank steak	30–40
Tuna	Salmon	20
Beef tenderloin	Steak au poivre	20
Swordfish steak	Swordfish kebabs	20
Halibut	Haddock	20
Chicken tenders	Chicken wings	15
Duck	Chicken	20–25
Sea bass	Trout	20–50
Chicken parmesan	Eggplant parmesan	15–20
Rack of lamb	Lamb roast	20
T-bone steak	Tri-tip	30–50
Veal	Pork	30–50
Foie gras	Chicken liver pate	50–60
Red snapper	Tilapia	33
Chicken salad	Greek pasta salad	50
Greens and Grains		
Polenta	Couscous	20
Asparagus	Green beans	10
Ravioli	Lasagna	20
Torta (Italian quiche)	Spanikopita	20
Risotto	Rice pilaf	15–20
Mesclun greens	Boston lettuce	50
Broccoli rabe	Broccoli	33

- **Stay seasonal.** Have a hankering for steamers at your October wedding? Sure, it's possible to get 'em, but it will cost you up to 50 percent more than it would when they're in season. It's best to stick to the order of nature and you'll save a bundle—and eat better-tasting foods. To find out which veggies are in season when, log on to http://www.nutritiously gourmet.com/html/produce.html.

- **Know your kebabs.** Serving kebabs can be a wonderfully tricky way of drawing oohs and ahhs out of your crowd while also feeding them more savvily. A kebab has *impact*. But it also has less meat than a straight steak. When it comes to tuna, serving it in a kebab instead of a filet can save you up to 50 percent. That's because kebabs tend to be made of leftover pieces of meat that are of the same quality. However, in smaller chunks, butchers and fishmongers can't unload them at the same rate. Hence, the savings are passed on to you!

- **Go heavy on the hors d'oeuvres.** Right after the ceremony, when guests are famished and eager to toast you heartily, is when you should go out with your A game. Put your umph into hors d'oeuvres, and you can go a little lighter on the quality of your entrées. "That's what guests remember," concludes wedding planner Barbara Howard.

- **Prettify your presentation.** Playing with the presentation of your food could actually allow you to pare down your final food costs. Amanda Hesser got playful when planning her menu: "We wanted it to be a progression: first course, eat with hands; second course, chopsticks; third course: fork; fourth course: long, thin milkshake spoon." Now, this might not have been the most budget-friendly menu, but you can incorporate the creative parts of Amanda's menu and serve simple foods with higher impact. For example, when people tuck into food using chopsticks, they immediately feel like they're having more fun than when they use a fork.

• **Curb the choices.** Your first step: Tune out the shrill voices coming from the peanut gallery. "We really set our minds on throwing a party celebrating our wedding, not a wedding," explains Amanda Hesser. "That small shift in definition helped. We felt no pressure to have favors, no pressure to have a cake, no pressure to do anything we wouldn't normally do at a dinner party. Everyone has an opinion and will freely throw it into the bucket: 'Uncle John has to have his scotch, Aunt Sue loves petits fours.' It was white noise to us. We shut it out." In a wonderfully firm twist, she decided that they wouldn't provide options, serving only lobster as the main entrée. "And my father-in-law is allergic to lobster. We figured those who didn't want lobster would make do. You're building in an expensive buffer just to give people a choice." To give a sense of how many people usually take that choice, Amanda found that only three of the 165 guests didn't eat the lobster. And those who opted not to eat lobster were able to munch on appetizers and sides. Not bad.

Cake Costs

When we started shopping around for a cake, I figured that we would just decide whether we wanted a $200 cake, a $400 cake, or a $600 cake. How wrong was I? Yet again, the wedding industry took me by the sleeve, shook me good and hard, and schooled me about how it's really done.

Wedding Chic Word to the Wise: Don't Do Dessert

At any other meal, you'd feel a little odd leaving your guests with just an appetizer and main course. "OK, thanks for coming. Talk to you soon!" "Er, what happened to dessert?" they mutter to one another as they all walk out the door, puzzled.

Sure, at other events that might make you a negligent hostess. But at this meal, it's not bizarre at all because of one major difference: You're serving a cake! In my mind, cake qualifies as dessert.

At our wedding, in the early stages of planning, my mother really wanted to serve fancy chocolates at the table. After a few months of back and forth, I talked her down to serving mints, and then, weeks before the wedding, I successfully talked her down to serving nothing at all. The fact of the matter is that I have been to dozens of weddings where dessert was served, or where trays of petits fours graced tables, and it all sits untouched. It seemed like such a waste, all those gorgeous desserts coyly calling out to totally uninterested guests. Allocate your funds for a delicious cake rather than spreading your funds thin with different dessert choices. They might be delicious, but they're destined for the trash or for being only partially nibbled.

In the wedding world, cakes are sold by the slice. You're having a wedding for 150? That'll be about $4 a slice, on average. So, um, four times 150 equals . . . carry the two . . . And that mental arithmetic is precisely why they price it like that—$4 sounds a lot friendlier than $600.

The most annoying part is that in addition to exorbitant per-slice fees, many bakers will tack on additional hidden costs. Breaking down the fees helps make an unpalatable price go down easier; once you take out the calculator, you find yourself gulping. Before contracting with a baker, ask if they charge extra for:

- Delivery (can be up to $150)

- Assembly (can be up to $25)

- Separators (can be up to $35 each)

Hidden Cost: Cake Cutting

If you think you can have your cake and eat it, too, you're forgetting one step: the cutting of the actual cake. And that's one thing that's far from sweet when it comes to your nuptial dessert.

Many venues or caterers might try to slip in an added charge, a "cake-cutting fee." The charges can start as high as $1.50 a slice. Now, I don't know what kind of fancy cutting they might do, but they'd better be cutting with gold knives to merit such a pricey surcharge.

Better than just forking over the dough, it's best to squash the unnecessary fee. "I don't think they should charge anything," concludes Sylvia Weinstock, baker extraordinaire in New York City, who has made cakes for the weddings of Cyndi Lauper, Donald Trump, a smattering of Kennedys, Christie Brinkley, and many more. "They should be honored to have our cake to cut." Amen.

Well, if you find that your caterer or venue is simply not prostrating themselves at the foot of your beautiful cake, you do have options. First, don't take it as the gospel, advises Sheila Himmel, a food writer at the *San Jose Mercury News*. You should absolutely negotiate this fee.

My favorite technique involves playing the aggressive "Hint, hint" referral card. For example, this line generally tends to get things started: "Well, I understand where you're coming from, sir. Of course I do. *Of course.* I'm just thinking how upset this makes me to have to pay what I consider to be an unnecessary charge. And then, well, how my fabulously wealthy friend is looking for a place for *her* wedding, and well, I love this place but I can't get past that fee. . . ." Bat the old eyelashes, look down, and wait for the response you want. "OK, I'll have to ask my manager, but I think we might be able to work something out."

Bingo.

Who Knew?

Legend has it that those who cut the cake and then smear it all over each other's faces are bound for divorce. Think about it. Who do you know who did the cake smear? Be nice. Feed gently, lovingly, sweetly. And don't—whatever you do—try the airplane-flying-into-the-mouth move.

Trim the Fat in Your Cake Costs

When planning your wedding cake, you can make some wise choices that will be both stylish and budget-savvy. Consider these tasty strategies:

- **Sneak in a decoy.** If you have a smaller, beautiful cake that you can cut for the photo op—or even craft a fake cake—

you can save major costs. Have the eye-catching cake (fake or simply small) on display, and then delicious sheet cakes waiting in the wings. No one will be the wiser, as waiters quickly whisk out the precut slices moments after you feed each other the tasty bites.

• **It's hip to be square.** When it comes to wedding cakes, you might have your sights set on a multitiered round Tower of Pisa in cake form. But the plain fact is that square cakes feed more people than round cakes. If you can find a home baker willing to charge by the cake rather than by the serving, you can save oodles by creating 90-degree angles in your confections. For example, fourteen-inch round cake will serve 75 to 80 guests, while a fourteen-inch square cake will serve 80 to 100 guests, according to the website baking911.com, run by Sarah Phillips, author of *Baking 9-1-1.*

• **Stay simple.** Neapolitan is a no-no, as is a cake with ten multifaceted layers. If you're not going for broke, you'll want one flavor and color for the whole cake, and as few tiers as possible so you don't have to pay for separators. "Each time you have to mix something up, you'll pay," says Condra Easley of Patisserie Angelica in Sebastopol, California, and an instructor at the Culinary Institute of California. If you really fancy some pretty touches, keep them to the smallest top layer, and just have the rest frosted in basic buttercream with simple piping. Going in the opposite direction, opting for all sorts of detailing, like sugar flowers and 24-karat edible gold hand-painting on the cake (hello?!), can double or triple your final cake costs.

- **Go for the real deal.** In an unlikely twist, real ingredients and embellishments will be far less expensive than edible fakes. For example, a fake fondant ribbon wrapping the cake requires real skill to make, as opposed to a real ribbon that you could just drape over as décor. Also, real flowers (if they're in season) can be far more affordable than sugar flowers. See if your baker will let you supply the details so that you can shave even more costs from her fee.

- **Cut the cake, literally, from your wedding menu.** Not every single wedding needs a cake. Your I do's will still be equally legit without the final kicker of cutting through fat slices of buttery baked batter. If you're not inclined, don't worry about it. Do what feels right for you. Amanda Hesser opted against serving a wedding cake, instead feeding her guests a plum compote with shortbread in tall glasses. "I'm not that big of a cake person," she says simply. Stay with

Wedding Chic Word to the Wise:
Give Up the Groom's Cake

A tradition that originally started in the South, groom's cakes are small confectionary mementos that pay tribute to the groom's interests. Bottom line? They're a waste of your money. Include him in the planning throughout, and he won't need a token cake in the shape of a shotgun, Maserati, or other outward sign of testosterone to counter your girly, pink, ten-tiered affair.

what feels good to you rather than what the wedding industry dictates. After all, remember that this is your event; you don't need to satisfy the industry. When someone inevitably moans, "You neeeeed

cake! You're not having cake?!" simply smile, nod, and politely describe the delicious dessert you will be serving. Period.

Wedding Chic Word to the Wise: Cut the Cake

Who says a wedding isn't legit unless you have a three-tiered confection covered in buttercream? Modern brides might have a hankering for something a little different, a little more personal. Here are some other options:

Cute and fun cupcakes

A fruit tart, a fresh dessert people always love

Sorbet, a light and refreshing treat at the end of the night

Ice cream with fresh berries always has takers

The 411 on Frosting Choices

ike the plethora of flower choices, you'll soon be swimming in frosting lingo. Marzipan ... ganache ... *God bless you*. Don't worry if you don't know the difference between buttercream and fondant. Here's the simplified scoop on what you need to know about the options in wedding-cake frosting:

Buttercream: basically a mixture of butter and icing sugar. Easy to flavor and color. And tasty. *Mmm-mmm.*

Fondant: made of sugar, water, and cream of tartar. Fondant is also known as sugarpaste. It has a silky look to it. The final word on fondant: "Forget it," says Sylvia Weinstock, New York City–based cake baker to the stars. The pricey frosting, which generally adds $1 to $2 more to each slice than buttercream, is inferior, she decrees. In Weinstock's experience, fondant generally covers buttercream anyway, and guests always end up peeling off the fondant to get to the good stuff. "I *only* use buttercream," she adds.

Ganache: made from chocolate and cream, the embodied fantasy of chocolate lovers everywhere.

Marzipan: similar to fondant but sweeter. Made from almond paste, icing sugar, and egg whites. It's great for making cake decorations, like fake flowers or fruit. It's best to use in piecemeal, because as total frosting, marzipan can tack on $1 a slice more than the price of buttercream.

The Contract Basics

Before signing, make sure the following points are addressed in your contract:

- The date, time, and address of your event.

- The name and contact info for your caterer.

- The number of servers who will be working at the venue.

- The clothing requirements for the caterer and servers.

- The hours you will have the servers for.

- The hourly fee for overtime.

- A specific outline of all fees (including a breakdown of costs and whether taxes and gratuities are included).

- Menu details, including flexibility for guests' special dietary needs (if relevant).

- The specifics of setup and clean-up.

- The deposit due date and balance due date.

- The cancellation and refund policy.

The Bottom Line

- Figure out what kind of food you'll need to serve based on the timing of your event. Events that take place earlier in the day are always cheaper.

- Be creative about where you look for a caterer.

- Don't be fooled! Buffets aren't always cheaper. The more choices you offer, the higher your costs will be.

- Plan a money-saving menu by making savvy food substitutions.

- Choose ethnic and seasonal foods for good prices, and go heavy on hors d'oeuvres.

- Curb your cake costs by choosing the most cost-effective (and tasty) frosting.

- Don't do additional desserts. A delicious wedding cake is plenty.

10 · The Drinks:

Settle on a Booze Budget
You Can Toast to

*U*nless you're a teetotaler or in recovery, a wedding doesn't feel festive without the easy flow of wine, champagne, and cocktails. You might truly care about the cake colors, the way your hair is done, and the band's outfits. But frankly, save for a few dry or preggers friends of yours, most of your guests will be focused on one main aspect of the reception: the cocktail choices.

Everytime I go to a wedding, I'm psyched to scope out the alcohol situation. "Excellent! Top shelf, open," my friend Lisa and I concluded at our friends Dave and Emily's Ann Arbor Labor Day event. "Nice! Limited, open all night," Michael and I noted at a friend's recent event. It's become a sort of shorthand for assessing the quality of a wedding bar.

When planning your own event, you quickly realize just how nauseating alcohol costs can become. Sure enough, booze is one of the fastest ways to drop dollars in a wedding. But don't resign yourself to serving green tea and sparkling water. It is absolutely possible to cap your cocktail costs in style. The choices are intoxicating.

Be Savvy About How You Set Up the Structure of Your Bar

*Y*es, of course, it would be nice to have an open bar all night long. Hot men pouring in crystal tumblers. Feeding guests grapes, one by one. Rare vintage wines. Shaken "It" cocktails flowing endlessly. And throughout, you'd have a pleasant, perfectly calibrated buzz—not too woozy, not too harsh.

And then you wake up and realize you'll need to contain your cocktail costs. The smoothest way to do that is to structure your bar arrangement wisely. There's a lot of ground between an all-night open bar and no bar. And the choices you make about what you want to serve, how long you serve it, and where will drastically affect the bottom line of your bar bill.

Your goal will be to make it seem like the above fantasy, while pulling off something a wee bit more affordable. When folks will notice it most, at the beginning of the night, the drinks will be flowing. Then, as the festivities taper off, the bar will become quieter and close.

The Bar Basics

There are three standard ways you can set up your bar:

1. **Open bar.** Guests come and ask, and they shall receive.

2. **Limited bar.** Guests come, ask, and are steered toward a smaller selection of options, and they shall receive.

3. **Cash bar.** Guests come, ask, and receive, and then they open up their wallets. (*Note*: This is not an option. Under no circumstances should you ever—ever!—subject your guests to a cash bar. If money is a serious object, cut in other places and keep a supremely streamlined bar so that you will at least have wine and beer. Even the unclassiest option, a keg, would be better than a cash bar.)

Within these choices, however, there are an endless number of ways that you can choose to structure your bar. You can keep things chic while also containing your costs. The budget-savvy bride will want to steer herself toward the limited bar. I like to think of it as the Limited Deluxe Bar.

At my wedding, we had a Limited Deluxe. During cocktail hour, we had mid-shelf open bar for an hour. Then the rest of the night, we served beer and wine. During our toasts, we served a nice champagne, and then, throughout the evening, guests were welcome to go up to the bar and enjoy beer and wine. There were no complaints. In fact, my friend Megan later told me it seemed like we had "bought out a winery," the bottles were flowing so liberally throughout the night.

Beyond the basic structure of open, limited, and cash bars, there are different ways you can pay for your bar. Here are some general guidelines. At different kinds of venues, you can pay in a variety of ways. You'll want to negotiate with the coordinator or caterer about what to do. Don't give in too easily on this one, because it could account for a difference of thousands of dollars in your bar bill. You could pay:

> ### Who Knew?
>
> Your best option for your bar bill will be to work it out with your caterer so that they let you bring in your own beverages. You'll pay a flat fee per head for glassware, napkins, ice, all the fixins (usually about $2 to $3 per person), and the bartender ($20 to $25 an hour), and you take on the challenge of rounding up the rest.

On consumption. Whatever your guests drink, you'll pay for. Good for a mixed crowd you don't expect to drink very much.

Per head. You pay a flat fee based on how many guests will attend your event. This is the all-you-can-eat-buffet model of bars. Good for a younger crowd that's likely to befriend the bartenders.

Up to a capped limit. You can have a limited open bar up to a certain amount that you decide on ahead of time, like $1,000. At that point, the bar either closes or partially shuts down to just beer and wine. Good for relatives you don't trust not to overdo it.

Per hour. You pay per guest, per hour. The prices descend as the night rolls on. For example, if you start off at $10 a guest per hour, the price generally drops to $5 a guest for the second hour and $3.50 a guest for each additional hour. Good for a reasonable adult crowd.

General Cost-Saving Strategies

eyond structuring your bar in savvy ways, you still have a plethora of options about how you can cap your costs. These choices are great because they seem like treats for your guests while ultimately being kind to your bottom line.

1. **Choose one or two signature cocktails that you can have bartenders steer your guests to.** My friend Emily had her guests drinking mojitos at a summer wedding. The beauty of the signature cocktail is that you only need to buy a few bottles of alcohol rather than stocking up on everything from tequila to gin only to find out at the end of the night that not one person asked for a margarita.

2. **Have a limited open bar.** Keep your bar open all night and you'll pay for it—for years to come. But you can have your bar open for a set amount of time (say, during cocktail hour, or for two hours of dinner, etc.), and cap your costs. The fact is that by the bitter end of the night, people won't be savoring their drinks as much as they were right after your ebullient I do's. Concentrate your cash on the beginning of the boozy evening rather than the end.

3. **Have a cocktail forty-five minutes instead of a cocktail hour.** Why must you be set on sixty minutes for the cocktail

session? One bride I spoke with noted that her cocktail hour extended for ninety minutes and that her bar bill at the end of the night was bloated because of it. If you don't give folks anything to do except stand around and pound 'em back, that's exactly what they'll do!

BYOB Wedding

hen planning their wedding in Pittsburgh, Pennsylvania, Seth and Dana were trying to contain costs while also keeping their standards high. A cash bar was completely out of the question for Seth, who had moaned about being at weddings where you had to have one hand on your wallet the whole time. So trashy! So when it came to figuring out how to structure their own bar, they did their homework and found a local liquor store where they

could buy what they wanted on discount and return whatever remained at the end of the affair. It worked perfectly for them.

The wisest way to contain your costs is to have a BYOB wedding. No, not one where guests bring their own alcohol (though our friend Jacob did score major points by sneaking in a choice bottle of Macallan for toasts at our wedding party table!). Instead, try to do some alcohol

bargain-hunting and stock your own wedding bar, like Seth and Dana, who managed an A+ bar at BYOB prices. Like us, they were stunned by how little their guests actually drank, and they were able to recoup a lot of the initial cost.

The best part about buying alcohol yourself is that you don't have to pay all sorts of surcharges. In general, venues can double the prices of alcohol. For example, that bottle of Stoli vodka will be $80 at the country club and only $40 at your local liquor store. And if just one guest requests a vodka tonic and the bottle remains 80 percent full at the end of the night, too bad for you. You're paying for every costly ounce.

The ABCs of Your BYOB Wedding Bar

1. Determine corkage costs, bottle-by-bottle savings, and your bottom line. Pull out the calculator. If it all computes, continue planning.

2. Find the best local alcohol discounter.

3. Figure out quantities (see guidelines on page 239).

4. Double-check the store's return policy to make sure you can get a full refund for unopened bottles.

Hidden Cost: Corkage Fees

Having a BYOB wedding—that is, supplying your own alcohol—isn't as easy as just borrowing a friend's van, stocking it, unloading it, and letting the games begin. Most venues tack on corkage costs for each bottle you bring in. In fact, I've even heard of catering companies that charge corkage fees for bottles that haven't even been opened.

Who Knew?

When it comes to corkage fees, the $10 to $50 per bottle charge isn't the end of the story. Believe it or not, corkage fees are subject to the same tax and service charge that your other catering fees are. That means you'll need to figure in tacking on an additional 18 percent for service and tax.

"Corkage fees are the restaurant or hotel's charge for money lost on you not buying the wine from them and to cover service for stemware use, labor, and possible breakage," explains Leslie Sbrocco, author of *Wine for Women: A Guide to Buying, Pairing, and Sharing Wine*. They can range from $10 a bottle to more than $50 a bottle. Sbrocco finds that corkage fees can be worth paying if you do your homework ahead of time and price things. For example, if you find moderately priced bottles of wine, and you get a discount for buying a case (which can be up to 20 percent), you can still pay a $15 a bottle corkage fee and come out ahead of where you would have been if you'd bought the wine through the caterer or venue. Even if the price works out to be the same, you'll be getting a better bottle for the same price range, the philosophy behind all your *Wedding Chic* actions. Plus, if you buy the wine yourself, you can bring home whatever remains when no one's left standing.

A Girl's Best Guidelines for Buying Her Own Alcohol

*T*he key to getting the best deal when setting up your bar will be tracking down the best budget liquor store. Spend some time scoping out the best bargains in your area. Look for:

- **The store's return policy.** It's not worth your while to stock up on discount drinks unless you're able to return what you haven't used for the full price. Find out what the return policy is before plunking down your plastic. Most stores won't let you return white wine that's already been chilled, so make sure to tell your bartenders to keep all but the essential bottles off the ice.

Wedding Chic Word to the Wise:
Nix BYOB Mixers

While buying your own booze—and buying wine is a wise move—don't try completing the task by picking up all the mixers, too. *Err, ten bottles of tonic, or should that be twelve?* "Make sure your caterer provides the mixers," suggests *Glamour's* Lynn Harris. "It would have been foolish for us to provide Sprite and Coke." That's what you pay the professionals for!

• **Package deals.** Constantine Mouzakitis, the proprietress of the chic wine bar Punch & Judy in New York City, says that "any wine/retail store will accommodate you when you're buying large amounts." She suggests ordering large amounts of one wine rather than providing a variety so you can get bulk discounts, which can save you 15 to 20 percent. Additionally, big-box stores and discount clubs like Beverages & More and Costco might have package-deal discounts, further cutting their already low prices. For example, Beverages & More sometimes has a "Buy a Bottle, Get the Next One for Five Cents" sale.

• **Local flavor.** Yes, the big-box stores might originally have lower prices on their bottles, but chances are you can work with your favorite local liquor store to get the same deals— especially when they find out the volume you plan to purchase. Lynn Harris, a contributing editor at *Glamour* magazine and the creator of Breakupgirl.net, did just that at her November wedding in Brooklyn. "We got a massive discount from our local wine shop because it's cheaper by the case. We bought the house wine that we drink anyway, so we don't mind having a couple cases around."

Standard Quantities

When purchasing your own matrimonial moonshine, you'll want to get the number of bottles right, even if you do have the flexibility to return what you don't use. After all, there's no sense in lugging extra crates, no matter how much it helps tone those back muscles.

You'll want to make sure you have enough so that no one will go with a glass unfilled—yet not so much that you have to worry about returning a vanload of bottles before blasting off on your honeymoon the next day. Like all other aspects of wedding planning, spirits are a science. Calibrate your cocktail costs! You can figure that:

- **One** bottle of wine will fill **five** glasses

- **One** bottle of champagne will fill **six** glasses

- **One** case of wine or champagne has **twelve** bottles

- **One** 1¾-liter bottle of liquor contains **forty** 1.5-ounce (strong!) servings

- **One** five-gallon keg equals **fifty-three** 12-ounce servings

- ¼ of all your guests won't be drinking (this number will be higher if you have lots of seniors, juniors, or those "with child")

- **One** drink every hour should be the average for your guests

Facts and figures are always nice, but what do they mean? Well, if you're planning on hosting 100 guests for a four-hour wine-only reception, you'll now know that you need five cases (seventy-five guests drinking a glass an hour). For any other calculations, you'll have all the tools you need to calculate reasonable figures. In general, if you want to stock a full bar for four hours, you can guesstimate that 100 guests will drink:

QUANTITY	LIBATION
2 cases	Beer
1½ cases	White wine
¾ case	Red wine (no one wants the spillage!)
1½ cases	Champagne (though most will remain in the flutes around the room, as people tend to forget about them)
3 bottles	Scotch/whiskey
1 bottle	Bourbon
2 bottles	Gin
4 bottles	Vodka
1 bottle	Rum
1 bottle	Tequila (though this should be the first to go if you want to pare down your bar—generally, it gets very few takers!)
1 bottle	Dry vermouth
1 bottle	Sweet vermouth

Top Shelf vs. Bargain Basement

*Y*es, Ketel One would be lovely, but if you're looking to shave costs, you might want to consider downgrading just a bit by only buying top-shelf bottles of your favorite kind of alcohol. For example, if you're a vodka-tonic girl, you might opt to invest in the best, premium-grade bottle of vodka and take it down a notch for the other kinds of alcohol. For punches, well bottles—the lowest-quality, no-name brands bars keep on their speed rack—could serve you best. The price range from high to middle to well is vast. Here's a sense of how much you could save, bottle for bottle:

TYPE OF ALCOHOL	PREMIUM	TOP SHELF	WELL
Vodka (1.75L)	Ketel One ($41)	Stoli ($36)	Smirnoff ($20)
Gin (1.75L)	Bombay ($40)	Beefeater ($35)	Gordon's ($15)
Scotch	Johnny Walker Black ($40/750ml)	Dewar's White Label ($40/1.75L)	Dawson ($21/1.75L)
Bourbon (1.75L)	Maker's Mark ($40)	Wild Turkey ($37)	Jim Beam ($23)
Rum	Appleton ($13/750ml)	Bacardi ($20/1.75L)	Castillo Gold ($14/1.75L)

Savings Breakdown

Vodka: save about 44 percent going with well instead of top shelf
Gin: save about 60 percent going with well instead of top shelf
Scotch: go with the good stuff here—yes, it costs about 35 percent more to

purchase premium instead of top shelf, but with something that people sip,
you want the quality to be top-notch

Bourbon: generally mixed, save about 40 percent going with well instead of
top shelf

Rum: save about 30 percent going with well instead of top shelf

Wedding Chic Word to the Wise: Your Boozehound Buddies

We thought our friends enjoyed their cocktails, so we planned to serve a lot of them. Hundreds. Thousands. We really had no idea how much folks would drink. So we estimated on the upper end. As it turns out, we must have considered our pals lushes, because they drank demurely. Michael's parents, who took care of the bar, recouped some of their initial investment by the end of the event. It turns out that our experience was normal.

"People overestimate the amount that people are going to drink at events," says Los Angeles–based event planner Harvin Rogas. Even if you think your friends and family can pack 'em away, think twice about how you structure your bar. Because our eyes were bigger than our guests' livers, we would have grossly overpaid if we hadn't been able to get the money back.

Bar Cost Breakdown

Your bar costs aren't made up of only the bottles of beer, wine, and booze you plan on stocking. Factor in the following when considering how much you will need to spend on your wedding bar:

- Bartenders (between $25 and $75 an hour and up, per bartender, plus tips)

- Waiters ($20 an hour and up, plus tips)

- Liquor (see above)

- Glassware (at least $15 to $25 per twenty-five glasses)

Should You Cut the Champagne Toast?

Certain things just say "weddings": white dresses, fluffy cakes, bickering with your boy—and champagne toasts. Right? Wrong! Since you're an unconventional bride searching out the nifty ways to make your wedding unique, chic, and affordable, this is one requisite part of the classic script you might want to consider putting the cork in. "I think people like champagne in theory," says Harvin Rogas. "We had champagne at a party recently for Paul Newman's charity, the Painted Turtle, a camp for chronically ill children. Nobody drank the champagne except for the one woman who kept insisting that we provide it. Everyone else wanted vodka."

Indeed, it's always worth your while to broaden your alcohol vocabulary beyond the three B's: booze, bubbly, and bud.

• **Serve an alternative to champagne.** For her bar options, Amanda Hesser served sparkling water, prosecco, and lemonade. Period. What was a wise move to limit bar costs also eliminated the need to ponder the champagne toast. They had a beautiful—often preferable—alternative to champagne in prosecco. Plus, she explains, "You can get a great bottle of prosecco for twelve dollars. And it's low in alcohol. We wanted to make sure that people made it to dessert. You go to those weddings where people have been drinking Cabernet Sauvignon during the cocktail hour. They're stumbling to the table and already full." Dale DeGroff, author of *The Craft of the Cocktail* and former bartender at the Rainbow Room in New York City, suggests Mionetto Prosecco Brut from Italy, which should run about $10 a bottle. Another option is a different champagne alternative: cava, Spain's version of sparkling wine.

• **Serve whatever floats your boat.** Why does it have to be champagne? In most other cases, the popping of the cork is our Pavlovian cue to Paarrr-tay. "We're celebrating now! The champagne is out!" But in the middle of your wedding, you're presumably already in that mode. No need to push the envelope here. Serve whatever you like.

- **Serve reasonably priced bottles.** "People feel like they have to get champagne like Veuve Clicquot or Cristal if they watch too much MTV," says Constantine Mouzakitis, owner of the New York wine bar Punch & Judy. "There are some amazing champagnes out there that are very inexpensive, just not as recognizable." Try Bouvet Brut from the Loire Valley, which generally costs $10 a bottle; Cristalino cava, which costs about $8 a bottle; or Pacific Echo from Mendocino, which costs about $13 a bottle.

- **Serve champagne cocktails.** Champagne cocktails are even more fun than the straight stuff. They add cute colors, extra fizziness, and a more festive vibe. But the secret behind champagne cocktails is that they can save you money. If you decide you want to have a champagne toast, consider serving cocktails. Why? You'll cut down on the cost of the champagne, because you're essentially using filler. And you can use a lesser-grade champagne because it won't be performing a solo act.

- **Serve sparingly.** If the champagne toast is a must, don't bother serving everyone teeming glasses. "People only have one sip and then there are all these half-empty flutes around the room," reasons Boston-based newlywed Angela.

The Best Budget Bottles

hen buying your wine, champagne, prosecco, or alcohol yourself, you'll need to have an idea of what you want. You can't just wander into a store with the directive, "Red, please." You'll need to bone up on the basics. The book *Wine for Women* is a wonderful resource, as is Andrea Immer's *Great Wine Made Simple*.

But if you'd like a quickie guide to great bottles, try some of these, which come highly recommended by Leslie Sbrocco and Dale DeGroff. A good rule of thumb? When in doubt, go with Australian wines, which are generally more budget-friendly:

Chardonnay: Yellow Tail, South Eastern Australia ($7 bottle)
Sauvignon Blanc: Brancott, New Zealand ($10 bottle)
Cabernet Sauvignon: Santa Rita Reserva, Chile ($12 bottle)
Cava: Cristalino, Spain ($6 bottle)
Champagne: Bouvet Brut, Loire Valley France ($10 bottle)

Chic Cocktails

It's fun to punch up your wedding bar by serving a signature drink. But consider what you serve wisely, because the majority of your guests will be enjoying it. Gin and tonics are always a nice option in the summer. But the *Wedding Chic* bride can get a little more creative than that. Celebrity bartender Dale DeGroff recommends serving something with vodka: "Vodka is always going to be mixed, so it's always going to have the flavor of something else, so you can get away with a less expensive vodka." But whatever you serve, give it a cute signature name, specified to your event: the Michaelina Mojita. The Forever After. The "I Do" Drink. The Wedded Bliss, with a cherry on top. Be vague so you can keep your guests guessing as to what's in the thing. The only thing they'll know is that they want another!

If you want to get a little fancy, which you can afford to do if you're serving a cost-saving signature drink, try some of Dale De-Groff's personal favorite drink recipes.

· The French Kiss ·

4 ounces vodka
1 ounce champagne (or prosecco)
1 strawberry

Combine, pour together, and enjoy.

· The Champagne Cobbler ·

8 chilled orange wedges
8 chunks of chilled fresh pineapple (cut into ¾-inch squares)
8 chilled lemon wedges
3 ounces Maraschino liqueur (have your liquor store order it from either the Stock or Luxardo company in Italy)
4 ounces Cointreau
One bottle of champagne (or prosecco)

Mash the fruit (which should be chilled) and the Maraschino liqueur in the bottom of a pitcher. Add the Cointreau and stir. Strain all the liquid from the pitcher, pressing the fruit to be sure you get all the liquid. Add that liquid to your punch bowl or another large pitcher and slowly add the chilled champagne. Stir very gently to avoid losing the bubbles, and serve. Float some thin wheels of fresh lemon and orange in the punch bowl. Voila! SERVES 6

· Casino Royale ·

1 ounce gin
1½ ounces of orange juice
½ ounce Maraschino liqueur
¼ ounce lemon juice
Champagne

Shake all ingredients except the champagne and strain into a
chilled martini glass. Fill with champagne and garnish with
an orange peel.

· Champagne Pick-Me-Up ·
(c/o Ritz Bar, Paris, c. 1936)

½ ounce VS cognac
2 ounces fresh orange juice
1 dash grenadine
Champagne

Pour together all ingredients, top off with champagne, and
enjoy.

The Contract Basics

*B*efore signing, make sure the following points are addressed in your contract:

- The date, time, and address of your event.

- The name and contact info for the bartender(s) who will be working at your event.

- The number of servers who will be working at your event.

- The clothing requirements for bartender(s) and servers.

- The number of hours you will have servers for.

- Hourly fees for overtime.

- A specific outline of all fees (including a breakdown of costs and whether taxes and gratuities are included).

- Details of the bar, including what will be served and who will be stocking it.

- Specifics of setup and cleanup.

- The deposit due date and balance due date.

- The cancellation and refund policy.

The Bottom Line

- Get creative with the way you structure your bar in order to maximize your budget.

- Try signature cocktails or a limited open bar to get the best of both worlds.

- If possible, save big by buying everything yourself (at a spot that accepts returns).

- Don't grossly overestimate or underestimate your guests' alcohol consumption.

- Figure out what's worth buying premium, top shelf, and well.

- Consider cutting out the champagne toast.

- Learn about wonderful, low-cost wines and chic cocktail options.

11 · The Odds and Ends:

Ensure That the Little Things Don't Drive You into Bankruptcy

*D*espite all your best intentions, your immaculately organized wedding binder, and your big stack of helpful magazine clippings, there's one thing that you can't plan for ahead of time: all the little expenses that pop up along the way. There are countless incidental fees and added expenses that are bound to become part of your budget. The best thing you can do is prepare for the ones you can anticipate—from license fees to officiant costs—by arming yourself with as much research as possible, knowing the range of what things should cost, and learning the markers of quality.

The Officiant

Average cost: about $300, but can go as high as $750

It's easy to get so wrapped up in the festivities (*Which shade of pink for the flowers?*) that you don't spend as much time mulling over small matters of the ceremony. Such as, well, *who* will marry you. Sure, you're raring to say "I do," but first someone has to ask the question, "Do you . . . ?" And you want to make sure the person standing in front of you has a kind demeanor, a firm grasp of your names, and doesn't perform the deed like a drive-through operation. Considering that this whole event centers on your union, it's worth investing plenty of time to track down the perfect person to unite you.

Who Knew?

Marriage license fees are not standard across the country. The smaller the county, the smaller the fee.

Wedding Chic Word to the Wise:
Paying Your Officiant

Depending on who you hire, you can expect to pay an average of $300 to the person who officiates at your wedding. But whipping out a fistful of twenties at such an occasion can feel a little crass. That's why many churches and synagogues request a donation to the house of worship instead of a fee paid directly to the officiant. If possible, try to pay your officiant in kind or make a donation. Michael and I were married by Larry Fine, a dear friend of his family who is a professor at Mt. Holyoke and who attended rabbinical school. Our premarital counseling consisted of a relaxing weekend at the Fines' house in Amherst, Massachusetts, laughing, talking about our future together, and eating delicious food. Paying Larry to marry us would have felt weird and inappropriate. Yet we still wanted to recognize him in some way. Instead, we made a donation in his name and gave him a rare book for his collection. He was perfectly pleased, and we felt we were able to compensate him in a meaningful way.

Finding Your Officiant

Even if you aren't religiously observant, that doesn't mean you have to head to City Hall to find a person qualified to marry you. Be assured: You have many options in searching out an officiant. Read on for a general list of who could do the deed:

A priest, rabbi, or other religious official

A judge

A justice of the peace

A notary public (in many states, you can save 10 to 15 percent on what clergy costs by hiring a notary public; to find out if your state qualifies, log on to http://usmarriagelaws.com)

Friends and family members (many states grant one-day deputy commissioner licenses to perform a ceremony; costs vary county to county)

Wedding Insurance

Average cost: anywhere from $150 to $500 and up, depending on a variety of factors

You don't hesitate to insure your house or apartment, and you can't possibly avoid insuring your car. So when making this equally enormous purchase, it's worth considering taking a similarly safe step. But before you run out and buy a big policy, familiarize yourself with the basics of your bridal backup plan.

Who Knew?

Some states offer discounts on marriage licenses (which range in price from $25 to more than $100, depending on the size of the county) if you and your intended sign up for premarital counseling.

What Is Wedding Insurance?

Wedding insurance is a policy you can buy that will partially compensate you if your wedding happens to be canceled for reasons outside of your control (see a list of examples below). *Note:* Cold feet does not qualify!

The price of a policy varies, depending on a wide spread of variables, including the location, time of year, size of the wedding, and so on. Laura, a bride in Chicago, paid $150 for $10,000 worth of coverage for her Florida wedding, which was taking place on the tail end of hurricane season. It ended up paying off.

"We figured we probably wouldn't use it, but it wouldn't hurt," she recalls. Well, it came in handy when the restaurant they booked a year and a half in advance for the reception shut down to make way for a condo development. "I ended up calling forty-five places, and only three were available. We had to book something more expensive than our first reception site, and our wedding insurance picked up almost all the difference between the two places."

What's Normally Covered

A delay caused by weather, rescheduling, or damage

One of your main people is a no-show for legitimate reasons (for example, injury or illness)

Loss of or damage to the photos (some policies will pay to have the VIPs reassemble for photo ops)

A last-minute problem with your dress (for example, if the store goes bankrupt)

Loss of deposits

What's Never Covered

A change of heart

Do You Need Wedding Insurance?

Of course, that's up to you to decide. But some folks are better candidates than others, embarking on higher risks for event cancellation. In general, you might want to seriously consider purchasing a policy if you fall into any of these categories:

You're getting married in the middle of winter in prime snow territory (i.e., where flights often get canceled, etc.)

You're having a destination wedding in a high-risk country

You're getting married in the Caribbean during hurricane season

A key member of your wedding party is seriously ill—or dangerously old

Tipping

Average cost: 6 percent of the total wedding costs, or about $1,300 for the average $22,000 affair

Sure, you agreed on a price and signed contracts with your vendors, but that doesn't mean you're exempt from recognizing a job well done. Obviously, if your caterer drops the ball, you're not exactly going to hand over a few extra hundred dollars in hearty thanks, but there are several people who will be working very hard to make this occasion exactly the way you want it to be. Decide in advance what you plan on giving, and then set aside separate envelopes and designate a close friend to distribute them. (Remember, you can always adjust the amount on the day of if something goes horribly awry or wonderfully well.)

All told, gratuities are far from gratuitous. They add up—fast! In fact, the total tally can be so high that you should make sure it's a line in your budget so you're not felled by the last-minute cash drain.

So how much cash should you take out of the ATM in advance? Below are some standard quantities and percentages.

THE PERSON	AVERAGE AMOUNT OR PERCENTAGE TO TIP
Venue coordinator/manager	15 to 20 percent
Hair and makeup artist	15 percent
Musicians	$20 to $25 and up per member
Delivery folks (flowers, cake, etc.)	$10 each
Photographer	$20 to $25
Food servers	$20 per server (give in bulk to the maître d' to distribute)
Bartenders	$20 per server (even if a service charge is included; it's a nice gesture)
Officiant	$300, preferably in the form of donation to a charity, church, or synagogue in the officiant's name

People You Don't Need to Tip

Unless they've truly bowled you over, a nice thank-you note will suffice for these folks:

Cake baker
Dressmaker
Jeweler
Stationer
Travel agent

Wedding Chic Word to the Wise:
Avoid Double-Tipping

Make sure that gratuities aren't included in the price you've set with your vendor before passing along a tip envelope. When it comes to caterers and bartenders, there is often a "service charge" included in the bottom-line fee. (Make sure to ask if that tip is passed along to the actual servers.) If you feel so inclined, you can always add to that, but you should know that it isn't necessary.

Wedding Rings and Bands

Average cost: varies widely, depending on the size of the stones and the type of metal

He may have made a solo decision on your engagement ring, but now you're making the joint purchase of your wedding bands together. And other than the photographs, your wedding rings are the only other major purchase that will be around after the honeymoon is over. So your decision (both aesthetically and financially) is weighty.

Choosing a Metal: The ABC's of Metals

Gold? White gold? Platinum? Who's to know? Consider these qualities of the major metal groups.

Platinum: Today's trendy choice. This metal surpasses gold in its strength, so you can feel quite safe knocking it around. Yes, you'll dent and scratch it, but you can polish it back to perfection, its strength will endure, and it will stand the test of time.

Yellow gold: The color you probably think of when you envision gold. It has the visual cachet of gleaming wealth. The quality is measured in karats (purity); 24-karat is pure gold, 14-karat is less pure. However, purer isn't necessarily best for a ring, since purer rings are softer and are easier to dent. In general, gold is softer than platinum and more easily damaged over time.

> ## Who Knew?
>
> Do you like the look of platinum but can't afford the pricey metal? According to TheKnot.com, white gold can cost approximately 45 percent less than its harder lookalike.

White gold: When gold is mixed with other alloys, the color lightens to white. However, note that it still bears the softness and malleability of its yellow sibling.

Many women like the looks of diamonds on their wedding bands, along with their engagement rings. While he may have selected the rock for your engagement ring, it's time to bone up on the difference between high- and low-quality diamonds. Consider it really valuable postgraduate work.

Choosing a Diamond: The ABC's of the 4 C's

When searching out a diamond, four criteria determine its quality—and therefore also its price.

Cut: The way the diamond is cut can render the most brilliant light reflections off its many facets. The better the diamond, the closer it comes to "ideal" proportions. The Gemological Institute of America (GIA) ranks diamonds' cuts from Class I (which is ideal) to

Class IV (the lowest grade). A smaller diamond may be more expensive if it is cut closer to the ideal, and it may seem more brilliant in the light.

Color: The clearer the diamond's color, the more brilliant it is. So unless you're planning to shell out millions for something approximating J.Lo's pink rock, you'll want to head to the whiter part of the scale. Diamonds' color is rated on a letter system. While D, E, and F are at the top of the scale in terms of being colorless, your naked eye isn't likely to detect too much of a difference between them and what follows (and is less expensive): those on the G, H, I, and J end of the scale, which are nearly colorless.

Clarity: Diamonds have all sorts of imperfections, most of which you can't see without a magnifying glass. Imperfections are also known as "inclusions," and they can be anything from cracks to scratches. The GIA rates diamonds' clarity on the following scale, from flawless to slightly included to imperfect: F1, IF, VVS1, VVS2, VS1, VS2, SI1, SI2, I1, I2, and I3. While you may want to go for perfection, it's worth considering that something from VS1 to SI1 can still be a very high-quality gem.

Carat: The weight of the diamond. One carat is the same as 200 milligrams.

Your Best Buying Decisions

Whatever the style or size of the bands you choose, there are some smart ways to go about making this purchase.

- Allocate 90 percent of your ring budget for a rock (if you're getting one) and 10 percent for the metal, advises Fred Cuellar, author of *How to Buy a Diamond* (Sourcebooks, 2004). Diamonds hold their resale value in time far more than metal, and they make a better investment.

• Be sure to buy a shape that is comfortable. A round ring can feel odd and uncomfortable for some fingers. I bought a ring that incorporates squarish angles from a store called Stuart Moore. The result is that it doesn't slide around. Many ring-shy men may find this more comfortable than a slippery round band.

• Go wholesale. The typical retail markup on rings is 300 percent, says Cuellar. Do a little digging in the Yellow Pages and look for wholesale retailers. (The diamond district isn't necessarily wholesale.) Alternatively, if you have a firm idea of what you want, try Costco or Sam's Club. It can take some time to weed through poor-quality merchandise, but there are diamonds in the rough. "I've seen some good deals there, but you have to look through a thousand diamonds," says Cuellar.

• Don't do eBay or estate sales. Unless you do this for a living, it's going to be very difficult to determine whether something is solid gold or schlock—especially on the computer screen. Leave eBay to the vintage shoe shopping.

• Go to great online stores you can trust, like www.Blue-Nile.com. Despite the leap of faith it takes to buy such an expensive purchase from a Web-based business, there are some really great deals to be found from reputable online retailers.

• Expand your horizon to gems other than diamonds. According to Gemworld International, prices for a one- to two-carat emerald range from $900 to $11,000; one- to two-carat rubies range from $975 to $12,000; and one- to two-carat blue sapphires range from $450 to $8,400. This can be much less than the price of a diamond of similar quality.

Who Knew?

Bundling purchases is always a good move, even when you're buying wedding bands. Try buying both his and her bands at the same place, and you're more likely to have bargaining power to reduce the final tally. Also, stores like Blue Nile.com offer discounts if you buy your engagement ring and wedding band both from them, even if they're not formally a set. Whatever you do, this is the time and place to bargain and negotiate.

• Consider refashioning a family heirloom. The ring itself could be an eyesore, but if there's a big rock enclosed in a bad band, it may be worth your while financially to have it either reset, recut, or removed altogether.

The Bottom Line

• Consider all your options for an officiant (notary public, friends, family, etc.).

• Ask about paying your officiant in kind, with a donation or gift.

• Get a marriage license in a smaller county to cut costs.

• Think about buying a wedding insurance policy if you're having a high-risk affair (old relatives, hurricane season, midwinter mountain location, etc.).

• Don't forget to tip.

• Reread your contracts to avoid double-tipping folks whom you're already paying a "service charge." (Be clear about who is getting what.)

• Go beyond the big stores for the best prices in wedding rings and bands.

• Buy both his and her bands together to negotiate savings.

• Learn quality markers in metals and gems.

• Consider gems other than diamonds to get the most for your money.

Part 3

THE POST-WEDDING BLISS

"My main advice? Don't spend a lot of time on this. If it's the focus of your life for a year, you're going to have post-wedding blues. I just wanted there to be decent wine. Every day of the honeymoon was better than our wedding day."

JOEL STEIN
WRITER • *Time* MAGAZINE

12 · The Honeymoon:

Slip into a Teensy-Weensy Bikini Without Losing Your Shirt

After all the brouhaha over whether you're going to import tulips from Holland, make all your bridesmaids wear halter tops, add a kosher Indian vegetarian option to your menu, and have Martin Scorsese involved in your videography, you're done. It's all over. You've walked down the aisle, done your Miss America wave, and kissed all your cousins good-bye.

Now comes the best part. Here's the time when it truly is just about you and your honey celebrating your union—preferably poolside with some fun cocktails in a land far, far away. Even if your budget means you need to stay closer to home, you'll still want to ramp up the relaxing and restorative touches.

When planning your wedding, however, it's easy to put off coordinating all the nitty-gritty details of the honeymoon. Other things seem so much more pressing—the dresses that came in a size too small (*oy!*), the battle brewing between the families (*ay!*), or the fact that your minister/priest/rabbi is MIA (*oo!*). But it's equally important—if not more so—to take a breather, pick up some brochures, hunker down on the Internet, and find your dream destination.

Like everything else, the range between high and low is huge. When Michael and I were trying to decide where we wanted to go, we were dizzied by too many choices. At the time, he was working at *Condé Nast Traveler,* so our problem was that we had way too much information. Our options were seemingly limitless. He'd come home with clippings from the current issue: Croatia! Saint Lucia! Tahiti! Then we started a spreadsheet on our computer, priced flights, and saw just how different the price of a trip to Crete and a trip to Cozumel would be.

More than the barrage of gifts, more than the amazing feeling of having all the most important people from all parts of your life come together to celebrate with you, more than any aspect of the actual event, the honeymoon is your reward. Set yourself up to savor it.

Travel Agents: Do You Need to Call in an Expert?

Sometimes even the savviest bride needs a little assistance. You might know flowers but come up short on your repertoire of hors d'oeuvres; you might have a great Rolodex of tailors but a dearth of information about key venue sites; and you might know absolutely everything about your hometown but dreadfully nothing about the island resort where you fancy touching down to celebrate your newfound Mrs. status.

That's OK. There are people out there who do. And the beautiful thing about seeking out help is that the best travel agents can actually get you better prices. Like wedding planners, paying a little money can save you even more. It's a delicate equation, and you have to do the math to figure out when it becomes worth it. But here's the basic formula: agent's fee − savings = bottom line. If the number is negative, it's time to say, "Sign me up!" If it's positive, negotiate or move on.

But how much do travel agents charge? It varies. Most get paid a 10 to 15 percent commission on the price of your vacation. That can feel steep, though, so it might be a better idea to look into alternative fee structures. Just pay for piecemeal guidance, like assistance finding a resort or help purchasing an airline ticket to a difficult destination ($25).

Travel agents are a good idea if:

- **You're heading into the great unknown.** Since Michael and I ultimately decided on going to the Greek islands, we figured we could use the advice of a pro. Our travel agent,

Angelique, who came recommended from one of Michael's former colleagues at *Condé Nast Traveler*, knew Greece like the back of her hand. She expertly guided us to the most beautiful, secluded spots. A week before our trip, she'd sent us a typed-out sheet with her favorite restaurants in our region. Yes, you might be short on time—and also cash at this point—but guidance like that is invaluable. Plus, since she specialized in the islands where we wanted to go, she was able to negotiate to get us free room upgrades. Why? They were

---

Wedding Chic Word to the Wise:
Search Out a Specialist

Just because your mom has used Estelle the Expert Travel Agent for twenty years to book all flights back and forth from Saint Louis to Dallas doesn't mean that you want to call Estelle to help you plan your honeymoon in Hawaii. To get the best service, you'll want to find a travel agent who either specializes in honeymoons or specializes in the region that you plan to visit. That way, the agent can get you the best deals. *Condé Nast Traveler* publishes a list of the best and brightest travel agents in their August issue each year, breaking it down region by region. That's where we got our supersleuth, and she saved us a lot of money, getting us very good value every step of the way. You can access much of the information in the magazine online at www.concierge.com.

places she sends many clients to, so she had bulk buying power, which we—as individuals—never would have had otherwise.

• **You've decided to go for a package deal.** You can shop around all you want for a package deal, but the fact of the matter is that those in the biz can get you a better rate than you could ever negotiate.

• **You tend to get nervous about potential catastrophes.** Even though Michael and I thought we had accounted for every aspect of the honeymoon, two days before we left, Olympic Airlines went on strike. How did we know? Our travel agent called us after she had spent hours on the phone with the airlines, arranging—and rearranging—alternative flights in case the strike infringed on our departure. Having a travel agent is psychological insurance. If something goes wrong, you can call someone who can make it better. (Additionally, travel insurance—which costs a couple hundred dollars, depending on where and when you're traveling—is a worthwhile investment, considering how much you're planning to spend on this trip.)

City vs. Chill: Choosing Your Type of Destination

Chances are, after you come out of this whole wedding flurry alive, the last thing you're going to want to do is tackle the Louvre in the morning and the Musee D'Orangerie in the afternoon. A honeymoon in Paris might sound romantic, but you must be realistic about what you're going to want to do. If you're like most newlyweds, that means one thing: serious chilling.

When Michael and I touched down on the island of Santorini in Greece, it was all we could do to leave the exquisite resort we were staying at to go watch a sunset in town. The extent to our decision-making capacity was simple choices such as (1) beach or pool, (2) magazine or novel, or (3) wine or beer. This was about all we could handle. After months of making decisions between shades of pink,

Who Knew?

International destinations generally hike honeymoon prices by about $1,000. And newlyweds who choose to head to the South Pacific or Asia spend the most on their dreamy getaways.

Wedding Chic Word to the Wise: The Hype of Hurricane Season

When I was planning our Labor Day weekend wedding, one thing I didn't consider—at all—at the time was how that date would affect our honeymoon choices. But sure enough, when it came time to create a list of destination options, I quickly discovered a surprisingly limiting factor: weather. When envisioning my honeymoon, there were certain essential requirements: gently lapping waves on white-sand beaches; infinite-edge pools; flip-flops 24/7. But I was forgetting one factor . . . the weather. Sure enough, in September, many classic honeymoon destinations are riddled with rain.

Continued

All of a sudden, every time I would decide on the dreamiest destination, my fantasy was thwarted with two words: hurricane season. It seemed like the hurricane season was just one year-round tsunami wreaking havoc in all the best spots. And we were scared off.

The upshot of the hurricane season is that prices cool down as well. And some risktakers among us don't mind trying their luck. David Kaufman, a freelance travel writer for *Wallpaper* and *Travel + Leisure* magazine, notes that the chances of having to stay indoors the whole time are super-slim. "There's only the threat of a hurricane. It's very rare that you'll be caught all of a sudden in a storm. . . . I went to the Caribbean five times this year during the hurricane season." On average, it rained about an hour a day. Consider it naptime, anyway. "People have the perception that when you get there, it rains for twenty-four hours straight. That's just not true. It means that it *might* rain."

cuts of chicken, and song playlists, the ultimate luxury is simply lying down in a padded deck chair, being served delicious foods, and dipping into a pool occasionally to cool off.

The bottom line is that while you might enjoy a full dose of culture, most people don't find the honeymoon to be the best time to cram in museums, theater, and city tours. Michael and I took one day trip away from our resort to see an amazing archaeological site on a neighboring island. It left us feeling like we weren't just sacks of Jell-O, that we were somewhat active. But it didn't take away from our general state of relaxation.

Tricks to Timing Your Trip

For the same reason that hurricane season drives down prices with the threat of relentless rain, prices around the world wax and wane with the seasons. But instead of simply going from high to low, there's a secret third—affordable—plateau in the middle. It's called a "shoulder season." A little less ideal than prime-time, and far more appealing than cold, rainy low season, the shoulder season is a series of weeks surrounding the high season, when things have cooled off just a teensy bit. Traveling during the shoulder season is like buying your bread from a bakery at the end of the day, when they discount the morning's goods. It might not be as fresh as you'd get in the morning, but it's certainly not so much worse that you'd turn down the discount. The quality is 99 percent there, and the discount is far more valuable than that 1 percent.

> ### Who Knew?
>
> Although you might be under the impression that the whole Caribbean is out of the question during hurricane season, think again. There are spots that are blissfully beyond the border of the windy, rainy threat: the ABC islands (Aruba, Bonaire, and Curaçao), as well as the easternmost islands, including Grenada, St. Vincent, Trinidad & Tobago.

The best budget bride can score fantastic deals by finding out which locations are in the midst of their shoulder seasons when shopping around for honeymoon destinations. When Michael and I went to Greece the second week in September, it was shoulder season. What did we experience? Clear blue skies, 80-degree weather, and slight afternoon breezes. Not to mention savings we wouldn't have received if we'd gone a few weeks before, in peak season, when we would have been experiencing the same exact weather. When else can you get a bargain for the same experience?

Your first step is to find out when various parts of the world generally have their shoulder season. Refer to this handy calendar, which identifies how you can time your deals at some of the world's most popular honeymoon destinations.

The Caribbean

$ Low season: early June to late October

$$ Shoulder season: mid-April through the end of May, and early November to mid-December

$$$ High season: mid-December through early April

Who Knew?

Heading to Hawaii in high season? It's a little-known fact that even though you're paying peak prices, you'll also find yourself in the middle of that area's rainy season. What gives? Find the best rates—and best weather—in October.

Hawaii

$ Low season: early June to late September

$$ Shoulder season: early October to mid-December, and mid-April to late May

$$$ High season: mid-December to mid-April

Tahiti

$ Low season: mid-November to late April

$$ Shoulder season: May and October to early November

$$$ High season: early June to late September

Europe

$ *Low season:* *early November to mid-December, and late December to late March*

$$ *Shoulder season:* *early April to mid-June, early September to late October, and mid-December (around the holidays)*

$$$ *High season:* *mid-June to late August*

The Dreamiest Destinations

When Michael and I were planning to go to Greece, we didn't realize the quality of the company we'd keep. We thought, naïvely, that we would be having a unique, romantic, solo adventure. But we quickly learned otherwise. Once we got there, we kept bumping into oodles of other honeymooners, also from New York City, some of whom had used our same travel agent! Fortunately, being unique wasn't our primary concern. There is a reason that honeymooners tend to pick the same kinds of spots. They're beautiful. And on your honeymoon, you want a sure thing, not a risky resort. According to *Bride's* and *Modern Bride* magazines, which surveyed 3,500 travel agents around the world, these are the world's most desirable spots:

1. Hawaii (winning first place seven years running!). Within Hawaii, Maui takes the cake.

2. Mexico (Most newlyweds opt for Cancun and the Riviera Maya.)

3. Jamaica

4. Tahiti

5. Bermuda

6. Saint Lucia

7. Italy

8. Las Vegas

9. Aruba

10. The U.S. Virgin Islands

But just because those spots are popular doesn't mean the price is right. Making a top-ten list doesn't usually do a lot for lowering a region's price point. *We're Hot! Hot! Hot! Now we can charge an extra 10 percent.*

Thus, it's useful to know which are actually price-friendly destinations. They're beautiful—and affordable. And they're not popular—just yet! *Shhh.* The wonderful thing about this world we live in is that travelers can unearth treasures of destinations. So forget going to the standard spots you read about in the magazines every month. Say poo-poo to the popular, and carve out your own trail in the spirit of savings and style-seeking. Opt for destinations with the same allure and a pinch less cachet. You'll cash in on the unknown. Why stop comparison shopping now?

INSTEAD OF	HEAD TO
Jamaica	Vieques, Puerto Rico
Mexico	Honduras
Italy	Croatia
Maui/Kauai	Molokai

Continued

INSTEAD OF	HEAD TO
St. Lucia	Dominican Republic
Tahiti	Vietnam
Greece	Turkey (or Tunisia)
Aruba	Buenos Aires
The U.S. Virgin Islands	Panama
Spain	Portugal
The Colorado Rockies	The Canadian Rockies
Outer Banks, North Carolina	Vancouver Island

All-Inclusive vs. À La Carte

*T*he grand buffet of honeymoon destinations, the all-inclusive resort, lets you come, be served, and pay one bill at the end. What started as the Club Med model is certainly a popular option for many honeymooners. But it's especially important to do good research if you're interested in an all-inclusive. The *Wedding Chic* bride is particular about what she likes, and she doesn't like to sacrifice style, even if it saves her a few pennies—or a few hours of research time. No, she is more interested in finding out creative ways to get a better price on what she ultimately likes. An all-inclusive resort might be strong on the aesthetic of the pool area, but the service might stink; it might have a great breakfast but a lame minibar; and it might have wonderful grounds but unappealing rooms. In short, the tradeoffs can be huge and ultimately undesirable.

It's hard to have an individual experience, notes Ted Moncreiff, a senior editor at *Condé Nast Traveler*. "You miss out on a lot. Having paid for lunch in advance precludes you from trying the fish or taco stand down the street, which you might want to. They don't encourage you to explore your surroundings."

That said, there can be some circumstances in which they'd be an appropriate option for you. You might want to consider an all-inclusive if:

• **You're feeling super-duper cheap.** After your beautiful wedding, you're seriously so short on cash that you don't even want to think about food or any added charges.

• **You know exactly what you're interested in doing— and the resort can hook it all up for you.** For scuba divers (a pricey hobby), a resort that specializes in diving, and that includes all fees, can be a great option.

• **All you want to do is hunker down and stay put until you board the plane home.**

• **You're not that particular.** Just being on a pretty island is good enough for you. After planning all 1,001 aspects of your wedding, it can feel like a welcome respite not to have to make any more decisions. Dinner? Here. Activities? Right here. Nightclub? Err . . . here.

Insta-Clues: Is the Resort Cheesy or Chic?

When you're sitting at home, doing research about possible destinations, you might find yourself seriously challenged to figure out what the best spots are going to be. Buried in Post-its, Excel spreadsheets, and magazine articles, you sift through stacks of information, surfing the Web like a sponsored semiprofessional athlete. But websites are only so expressive about what resorts are actually like. Often, you will have to take your cues from small clues that speak a much larger message.

Michael and I ruled out one resort in Mykonos because its site used so much Flash programming that we felt like we needed to slip on our sunglasses. Then we noticed that the only photos of the re-

sort we could find focused on bronzed hotties around a pool, sipping some kind of cock-tail—always in a martini glass. There was not one photo of a room. And while we were certainly impressed with the resort's beautiful blue lighting under the pool area's palm trees, it was highly suspect that that was *all* they wanted to show. It seemed so aggressive in its attempt to be viewed as cool that we fig-

ured the resort would be filled with people who also just wanted to be viewed as cool. *Very uncool*, we concluded. Next!

In addition to curious absences of information, what are some other markers that can clue you in to what might turn out to be a bad resort? Beyond the obvious others—like (1) no pool, (2) once-weekly maid service, and (3) gift shops with stuffed animals in them—these are always tip-offs that you should keep an eye out for. Consider them Resort Red Flags. If they turn up, avoid them or go at your own risk:

• **Lace.** Presumably, the *Wedding Chic* bride is not looking for Ye Olde Victorian Country Inn Honeymoon. Overuse of lace is a chintzy, cheesy sign—especially if you can see any brown-ing around the edges.

• **Overly! Effusive! Praise!** If every comment posted on the resort's website is bursting with praise, push aside the initial instinct to see that as a wonderful thing and put on your skeptical hat, especially if they all adopt the exact same tone. Can you say . . . comments from the resort's marketing department? Nathan Lump, a senior editor at *Travel + Leisure*, says he finds negative comments much more useful. "They'll convey specific information like, 'One of the things I hated is that there are lots of kids around the pool.'" At least you know something more specific than, "Best time of my life! You haven't lived until you've come here!" Or some such other cliché.

• **Bedspreads.** Ted Moncreiff coordinates *Condé Nast Traveler's* Hot List issue, a compilation of the world's best resorts. He maintains that this is his number-one rule for deciding on whether a resort is worth visiting is if the beds have gross coverings on them. "It's all about the bedspread," he explains. "If there is a bedspread, you might want to look at another place. The standard now is a duvet with a down comforter—not a bedspread. I can tell from a bed if it's worth it to nix."

These are helpful clues in deciphering the bad, but how do you locate the good? Well, in addition to cashing in your number-one tool, referrals (Where did Sally and Sam go? What was that spot your coworker was raving about last week?), you can find some handy cheat sheets. For example, why not piggyback with folks who do this for a living? Find out where quality tour operators (like Backroads, Geographic Expeditions, and Abercrombie & Kent) are descending, suggests Nathan Lump of *Travel + Leisure*. The pros' criterion—reliability, beauty, and comfort—are surely what you're in the market for as well.

Give the Heave-Ho to Honeymoon Packages

One of the most fun parts of your honeymoon is actually getting to say, "We're on our honeymoon!" Everywhere Michael and I went, I would tell people, if they couldn't already figure out by the dopey grins on our faces. Among the reasons that I was so eager to announce the reason for our decadent vacation was that I was hoping people would treat us extra-special nicely, loading us up with bottles of champagne, treating us to food here and there, and cooing at us warmly. The truth is . . . many people do.

But although I was gung-ho about announcing our newlywed status once we were settled at our destination, I decided to keep it to myself when we were planning our vacation. Why? I wasn't interested in so-called "honeymoon deals." You'll find that resorts always have a honeymoon package with a "special" offer for newlywed guests. But it's a rare honeymoon package that actually saves you money.

In fact, in most cases, anything "honeymoon" is simply a reason to hike the price. For example, the typical honeymoon package includes some, if not all, of these components: champagne upon arrival, one "special" resort dinner, his and hers massages, a rental car, a tour of the area, a dinner cruise. Now, be honest with yourself: How many of those things would you be so excited about that you would actually pay for separately?

Massages? *Yes!* Champagne? *Yes!* Rental car. *Sure, why not?* Dinner cruise? *Err, pass.* Tour of the area? *Please.* But the fact is that packages are packages, and you end up paying for it all, not just the items you would want in the first place. And, surprisingly, honeymoon packages are often really bad deals if you sit down and price every component that you'd really want in the first place. Instead, take a moment to figure out what would really make it a wonderfully special vacation, and price those things separately. Chances are, your à la carte menu will be far more palatable than any preformed honeymoon package cocktail they assemble for you.

Great General Travel-Planning Tips

hether you're planning to honeymoon in Niagara Falls or New York City, the Amalfi Coast or Aruba, your own backyard or Bali, you'll still want to score the same kinds of deals. Consider these wise general strategies culled from travel pros who make a living in the travel biz:

• **Jump on good prices.** Shopping around is always well and good, but if you find a $200 flight to Bermuda one late, late night on the Internet, don't be a dope and sleep on it, hoping that tomorrow it'll drop to $180. A good price is a good price. Don't try your luck hoping for a better one. In twenty-four hours, the price of one flight can skyrocket.

• **Do your research.** Before you get your heart set on honeymooning in Vegas on one particular weekend, consider if there is a major reason why the hordes will be descending, which could make your life both unpleasant and unpleasantly pricey. Some reasons: a convention, a major sports game, or a cultural event. "You don't want to go to Telluride to ski and get away from it all if the film festival is going on," notes Dana Dickey of *Condé Nast Traveler*.

• **Try to anticipate what you'll really need.** You might think that you'll really want a rental car the entire time you're away, but the fact of the matter is that if you're heading to a ritzy resort, it's going to take a lot to entice you away from the grounds. Would you rather chill by the pool or drive twenty miles to check out some notable museum? However well intentioned you might be, it's likely your rental car will sit idle for days. If you're planning one or two day-trips, why not rent a car for just a few days rather than an entire week? Try to be realistic about what you're truly going to want to do. Almost everything remains at your primary destination—and starts with *s*: sleep, sun, swim, and sex.

• **If your budget is a primary concern, think mainland, not island.** The fact of the matter is that anything on an island is going to cost you more than it would on the mainland. And for good reason: Everything must be shipped in. But if your pennies are truly pinched, that might be reason enough to maximize your budget by avoiding islands altogether. "The more captive you are, the more they're going to nickel and dime you," explains Wendy Perrin, the consumer news editor at *Condé Nast Traveler*. "If you're on a private island and they're the only ones offering jetskiing, they'll charge you eighty dollars an hour or more."

Extras to Avoid at All Cost

Once you're firmly ensconced at your dreamy destination, you don't want to pour your pennies down the toilet. Yes, you're OK with splurging somewhat right now, but there are certain things that just aren't worth any price. Resorts hike prices on the items below at such a significant rate that they're just not worth your while. You may be in heaven, but don't let your head waft up into the clouds. Avoid these unnecessary extras:

- **Mini bar.** Just go to a corner store and stock up on what you're going to want so that you don't pay $5 for a bottle of water.

- **Phone calls.** Even local calls at a resort are insanely expensive. Think ahead and buy a prepaid phone card that you can use on a pay phone outside the room.

- **Last-minute toiletries.** You're going to be in the sun. Don't forget your sunscreen. Resorts just hope for forgetful folks whom they can charge $15 a bottle for sunscreen in the in-house gift shop. In fact, they're so psyched about it that they charge as much as three times the market rate. It's worth your while to take a moment when you're packing and try to think of everything you *might* need.

A Girl's Honeymoon Checklist

Once you're planted poolside, you'll want a certain stash of necessities—and little luxuries. Don't leave home without these items:

> ## *Wedding Chic* Word to the Wise: At-Home Honeymoons
>
> **Don't believe the hype! You don't need to fly fifteen hours to Bora-Bora in order to have a bona fide, romantic honeymoon. Many couples find it equally romantic and even *more* relaxing to stay at home after the big affair. Alex decided to take an at-home honeymoon, hiding out and chilling in a way that she and her husband never get to do. All of their friends were still going to be in town from the wedding, and they would get to spend some serious quality time. She treasured that as much, if not more, than the idea of dealing with flights, packing, and expensive foreign lands.**

Necessities

A copy of your wedding license (even if you booked the tickets in the bride's name—which is generally a good idea, paperwork-wise)

Passport

A variety of credit cards

Traveler's checks

Sunscreen!

Little Luxuries

A variety of lingerie

Multiple new bikinis (my favorite honeymoon score was a new Jean Paul Gaultier nautical-themed blue-and-white-striped teensy bikini I got at the Barneys Warehouse sale weeks before boarding our plane to Athens).

CDs (in your hotel room, you'll want to import a little . . . vibe)

Travel candles (just a small, lovely scented mini candle you can take out to turn your hotel from anonymous to A-list)

The Bottom Line

- Figure out if it's worth it to call a travel agent.

- Cash in on various regions' shoulder season for near-ideal weather and great prices.

- Avoid popular spots for similarly beautiful, but less frequented, alternatives.

- Ditch "honeymoon" packages with overpriced, unnecessary extras; go à la carte.

- Consider a stress-free option: the at-home honeymoon!

RESOURCES

Locate the best services and goods in your neck of the woods by consulting these organizations, associations, websites, and great books. They were super-handy resources for assembling all the information in this book!

PART I
The Pre-Wedding Planning

CHAPTER 1
Do You Need a Wedding Planner?

Association for Wedding Professionals International: www.afwpi.com; (800) 242-4461
Association of Certified Wedding Consultants: www.weddingconsulting.com; (800) 520-2292

CHAPTER 2
The Invitations: Share the Who, What, and Where, for the Right How Much

Carlson Craft: www.carlsoncraft.com; (800) 774-6848
Crane's: www.crane.com; (800) 268-2281
Kinko's: www.kinkos.com; (800) 2-Kinkos
Office Depot: wwy.officedepot.com; (800) Go-Depot
Paper Source: www.paper-source.com; (888) PAPER-11
Papyrus: www.papyrusonline.com; (800) 574-3906
San Francisco Center for the Book: www.sfcb.org; (415) 565-0545

www.einvite.com
www.invitationsbykarina.com
www.mygatsby.com
www.theknot.com
www.weddingchannel.com

CHAPTER 3

The Venue: Place Yourself in the Right Price Range from the Beginning

American News Women's Club, Washington, D.C.: (202) 332-6770
Brazilian Room, California: www.brazilianroom.org; (510) 540-0220
Brooklyn's Botanic Gardens: www.bbg.org; (718) 623-7220
Clise Mansion, Washington: (425) 865-0210
Earl Hall at Columbia University, New York City: (212) 854-1487
House of Blues Foundation Room at Mandalay Bay, Nevada: (702) 632-7600
Little Church of the West: www.littlechurchlv.com
Regal Rents: www.regalrents.com
Waldorf-Astoria: www.waldorfastoria.com

CHAPTER 4

The Threads: Be Queen for a Day Without Getting Royally Ripped Off

Century 21: www.c21stores.com
David's Bridal: www.davidsbridal.com
Discount Bridal Service: www.discountbridalservice.com
DSW Shoe Warehouse: www.dswshoe.com
The Fashion Book (Phaidon Press, 1998)
Filene's Basement, Massachusetts: (617) 542-2011
How to Buy Your Perfect Wedding Dress by Mara Urshel, Ronald Rothstein, and Todd Lyon
     (Fireside, 2002)
Kleinfeld: www.kleinfeldbridal.com (718) 765-8500
Linea Nervenkitt: www.nervenkitt.com
Nicole Miller: www.nicolemiller.com
One Night Affair: www.onenightaffair.com (310) 474-7808
Vera Wang: www.verawang.com
www.bridepower.com
www.bridesave.com
www.craigslist.org
www.eBay.com

www.ivillage.com
www.makingmemories.org
www.nearlybridal.com
www.nysale.com
www.rkbridal.com

CHAPTER 5
Head-to-Toe Beauty and Fitness: Beautify All You Want
Without Paying Too Pretty a Penny

Buff Brides: The Complete Guide to Getting in Shape and Looking Great for Your Wedding Day by Sue
    Fleming (Villard, 2002)
The Business of Bridal Beauty by Gretchen Maurer (Milady Publishing Co., 1998)
Los Angeles Beauty College: (213) 382-1300
Pacific Beauty College: (714) 839-1276
www.beautyschools.com
www.weddingchannel.com
www.weddinghair.com

PART 2
The Present: The Day-of Details

CHAPTER 6
The Tunes: Score Entertainers with Prices That Are Music to Your Ears

American Disk Jockey Association: www.adja.org; (888) 723-5776
New England Conservatory in Boston: www.newenglandconservatory.edu; (617) 585-1170
San Francisco Community Music Center: www.sfmusic.org

CHAPTER 7
The Flowers: Get the Most Bloom for Your Buck

California Commission on Cut Flowers: www.ccfc.org/flowers/flowers.html; (831) 728-
    7333
The Knot Book of Wedding Flowers by Carley Roney (Chronicle Books, 2002)
Price Chopper: www.pricechopper.com
Safeway: www.safeway.com

Society of American Florists: www.safnow.org; (800) 336-4743

USDA's Wholesale Cut Flower Price Reports: www.ams.usda.gov/fv/mncs/ornterm.htm

Whole Foods: www.wholefoods.com

www.2dozenroses.com

www.buyacandle.com

www.fischerandpage.com

www.flowersbulbs.com

www.marisolblooms.com

www.matternflwrs.com

www.theflowerexchange.com

CHAPTER 8
The Photos: Make Saving on Your Photographer a Real Snap

Professional Photographers of America (PPA): www.ppa.com; (800) 786-6277

Wedding Photojournalist Association: www.wpja.org

Wedding and Event Videographers Association (WEVA) International:
    www.weva.com; (941) 923-5334

www.theknot.com

www.perannum.com

www.proweddingalbums.com

CHAPTER 9
*The Eats: Create a Wedding Menu with Tastes and Prices
You'll Find Palatable*

Baking 9-1-1: Answers to Frequently Asked Baking Questions by Sarah Phillips (Simon & Schuster,
    2003)

California Culinary Academy: www.baychef.com; (415) 216-4338

Cooking for Mr. Latte by Amanda Hesser (W.W. Norton, 2003)

www.baking911.com

www.culinaryschools.com

www.nutritiouslygourmet.com/html/produce.html (Monthly Produce Calendar)

CHAPTER 10
The Drinks: Settle on a Booze Budget You Can Toast To

Beverages & More: www.bevmo.com

Costco: www.costco.com

The Craft of the Cocktail by Dale De Groff (Clarkson Potter, 2002)

Great Wines Made Simple: Straight Talk by a Master Sommelier by Andrea Immer (Broadway Books, 2000)

Wine for Women: A Guide to Buying, Pairing, and Sharing Wine by Leslie Sbrocco (William Morrow/HarperCollins, 2004)

CHAPTER 11
The Odds and Ends: Ensure That the Little Things Don't Become Hugely Expensive

American Gem Society: www.ags.org; (702) 255-6500

Gemological Institute of America: www.gia.org; (760) 603-4000

Gemworld International: www.gemguide.com

How to Buy a Diamond by Fred Cuellar (Sourcebooks, 2004)

Jewelers of America: www.jewelers.org; (800) 223-0673

Universal Life Church, for Do It Yourselfers: www.ulc.org

Weddingsurance: (800) 364-2433

www.bluenile.com

www.diamondhelpers.com

www.diamondregistry.com

https://usmarriagelaws.com (marriage laws by state)

www.weddingministers.com

www.wedsafe.com

PART 3
The Post-Wedding Bliss

CHAPTER 12
The Honeymoon: Slip into a Teensy, Weensy Bikini Without Losing Your Shirt

American Society of Travel Agents: www.astanet.com

Condé Nast Traveler (August issue)

www.concierge.com

General Information

Bride's magazine

Here Comes the Bride: Women, Weddings, and the Marriage Mystique by Jaclyn Geller (Four Walls Eight Windows, 2001)

The Knot's Complete Guide to Weddings in the Real World by Carley Roney (Broadway Books, 1998)

Martha Stewart Weddings magazine

Modern Bride magazine

The Nearly-Wed Handbook: How to Survive the Happiest Day of Your Life by Dan Zevin (Avon Books, 1998)

NYC Wedding Library: www.weddinglibrary.net; (212) 327-0100

Vows magazine: www.vowsmag.com

www.theknot.com

www.weddingchannel.com

INDEX

ABOUT THE AUTHOR

NINA WILLDORF is the author of *City Chic: An Urban Girl's Guide to Livin' Large on Less*. In addition to working as an editor at *Child* magazine, Nina also writes for *Entertainment Weekly, Modern Bride, Condé Nast Traveler, Real Simple*, and *New York* magazines. She lives in New York City with her husband.

Photo by Tess Steinkolk